White Elephant Gifts For Adults

500 SERIAL KILLERS ENCYCLOPEDIA

FACTS AND FIGURES

EXCLUSIVE BONUS

TEST YOUR KNOWLEDGE NOW!

K. MURDLE

PAPERBACK ISBN: **978-969-5492-80-2**

EXCLUSIVE BONUS!

Scan This Code to GET FREE COPIES of
500 SERIAL KILLERS Encyclopedia
Original SERIAL KILLERS Trivia BOOK
THE ULTIMATE TRUE CRIME TRIVIA

Table of Contents

INTRODUCTION 5

Chapter One: A-List 7

Chapter Two: B-List 31

Chapter Three: C-List 39

Chapter Four: D-List 47

Chapter Five: E-List 56

Chapter Six: F-List 62

Chapter Seven: G-List 67

Chapter Eight: H-List 75

Chapter Nine: I-List 81

Chapter Ten: J-List 84

Chapter Eleven: K-List 103

Chapter Twelve: L-List 107

Chapter Thirteen: M-List 115

Chapter Fourteen: N-List 125

Chapter Fifteen: O-List 128

Chapter Sixteen: P-List 130

Chapter Seventeen: R-List 134

Chapter Eighteen: S-List 146

Chapter Nineteen: T-List 152

Chapter Twenty: V-List 162

Chapter Twenty-One: W-List 167

Chapter Twenty-Two: Y-List 184

Chapter Twenty-Three: Z-List 189

Conclusion 193

Other Books in The Series 194

INTRODUCTION

Step into the grim pages of *The Serial Killers Encyclopedia*, where the most disturbing figures in history emerge from the shadows. This is more than a simple collection of names and statistics—it's an unsettling journey into the lives and minds of More or less 500 serial killers, each leaving behind a trail of fear, confusion, and devastation. Every killer cataloged in this encyclopedia has carved their own mark on history, exposing the horrific potential of human cruelty—calculated, relentless, and often beyond comprehension.

Within this collection, we encounter killers whose methods and motivations varied as much as their victims. Some were driven by deep-seated racial hatred or sinister cult ideologies, their acts reflecting a violent unpredictability. For instance, Joseph Christopher and Salvatore Perrone, who struck with their .22 caliber weapons, left a deadly imprint on the streets of New York years apart. Christopher's racially charged killing spree in the 1980s left 13 dead, while the Lewingdon brothers in Ohio, using the same caliber gun, took 10 lives in a chilling spree of random violence.

It's not just the high-profile cases that stand out. Lesser-known but equally terrifying figures like Ivan J. Hill—the 60 Freeway Slayer—who murdered six women, and Moses Sithole—South Africa's ABC Killer—who claimed over 38 victims, each left behind waves of terror that crossed cultural and geographical borders.

Some killers still remain elusive. The mysterious .25 Caliber Killer of New York was never brought to justice, leaving the unsettling question of whether they walk freely today. Meanwhile, the rumored 4Pi Movement—a suspected 60-member cult active between New York and California—adds another layer of fear, hinting at the darker possibilities of collective violence carried out in the name of ideology.

Internationally, killers like Abdallah al Hubal from Yemen, who claimed 13 victims over nearly a decade, and Abdullah Shah of Afghanistan, whose killing spree took 20 lives in the 1990s, highlight the global scope of serial murder. The dark nature of these crimes transcends borders, reminding us that the capability for such evil is a human phenomenon, not limited to any single nation or culture.

This glimpse is just the surface. Behind these cases are hundreds more—each killer with a twisted story of murder and mayhem. *The Serial Killers Encyclopedia* offers not only facts and figures but provokes deeper questions about the darkest sides of humanity. How does someone develop the capacity for such cold-blooded cruelty? Can society recognize these killers before it's too late?

What lies ahead is far more than a list—it's a confrontation with the darkest impulses in the human soul. As you venture through these pages, prepare to meet some of the most terrifying figures in history, each leaving an indelible mark on the world.

Chapter One: A-List

ABC Serial Killer

Aliases: None
DOB: N/A
Nationality: Argentine
Active Years: 1997-2004
Victims: 19 confirmed
Location: Buenos Aires, Argentina
MO: Shot and killed people randomly
Conviction: Unsolved

Brief biography:

The ABC Serial Killer is a still-unknown murderer who targeted people in Buenos Aires, Argentina, from 1997 to 2004. The killer's name comes from the fact that the first names of most of the victims corresponded to the letters A, B, and C in alphabetical order. He primarily targeted men in public spaces, shooting them in cold blood. Despite multiple investigations, the ABC Serial Killer has never been identified or apprehended, and the case remains one of Argentina's greatest unsolved mysteries.

Abdallah al Hubal

Aliases: None
DOB: N/A
Nationality: Yemeni
Active Years: 1990s
Victims: 20+ confirmed
Location: Yemen
MO: Shot and killed people, mostly in tribal conflicts
Conviction: Shot dead by police

Brief biography:

Abdallah al Hubal was a Yemeni gunman responsible for a string of murders throughout the 1990s, mostly related to tribal conflicts in the country. He was feared for his violent tendencies and ability to evade capture for many years. His murder spree reportedly claimed more than 20 victims. After several manhunts, al Hubal was shot and killed by police forces during a standoff in the late 1990s, putting an end to his reign of terror.

Abdelali Amer

Aliases: None
DOB: N/A
Nationality: Moroccan
Active Years: 2000s
Victims: 5 confirmed
Location: Morocco
MO: Rape and murder of women
Conviction: Sentenced to death

Brief biography:

Abdelali Amer is a Moroccan serial killer who was convicted of the rape and murder of five women in Morocco during the 2000s. His victims were found strangled, and in several cases, there were signs of sexual assault. Amer was eventually apprehended, tried, and sentenced to death for his heinous crimes. His case sparked widespread fear and outrage across the country, and it remains one of the most notorious in Moroccan criminal history.

Abdelali Hida

Aliases: None
DOB: N/A
Nationality: Moroccan
Active Years: 2010s
Victims: 3 confirmed
Location: Morocco
MO: Rape and murder of women
Conviction: Sentenced to death

Brief biography:

Abdelali Hida is a Moroccan serial killer convicted of murdering three women in the 2010s. His modus operandi included luring women into secluded areas, raping them, and then strangling them to death. His brutal acts shocked the nation, and he was quickly captured following a police investigation. Hida was sentenced to death and is currently awaiting execution. His case brought attention to issues of violence against women in Morocco.

Abdufatto Tashpulatovich Zamanov

Aliases: None
DOB: April 7, 1973
Nationality: Tajik
Active Years: 2004
Victims: 6 in one day, several more
Location: Krasnoyarsk, Russia
MO: Random attacks, robbery, murder with various objects
Conviction: Sentenced to life in 2008

Brief biography:

Abdufatto Zamanov was a Tajik-born serial killer who murdered multiple people in Russia, including six in one day. He committed random attacks in suburban areas and used improvised weapons to kill his victims. Zamanov was arrested in 2004 and sentenced to life imprisonment in 2008. He remains incarcerated at the Polar Owl colony in Russia.

Abdullah Shah

Aliases: None
DOB: N/A
Nationality: Afghan
Active Years: 1990s-2000s
Victims: 20+ confirmed
Location: Afghanistan

MO: Murdered civilians and rivals
Conviction: Executed in 2004

Brief biography:

Abdullah Shah was an Afghan warlord and serial killer responsible for the murders of over 20 people during the Afghan civil war and its aftermath. He was known for his extreme brutality, often torturing and killing his rivals, as well as innocent civilians caught in the crossfire of his rise to power. In 2004, after the fall of the Taliban, Shah was arrested, tried, and executed by the new Afghan government for his war crimes and murder spree.

Ade Family Murders

Aliases: None
DOB: Various
Nationality: American
Active Years: 1847
Victims: 5
Location: Madison Township, Indiana, USA
MO: Bludgeoning and decapitation
Conviction: Unsolved; no convictions

Brief biography:

The Ade family, consisting of Jacob Ade, his wife Pauline, and their three children, were brutally murdered in 1847 in Madison Township, Indiana. Some of the victims were decapitated, and their house was set on fire. The crime is believed to have been a robbery, as Jacob Ade was known to keep large sums of money at home. Despite an extensive investigation, the case remains unsolved.

Adil Albani

Aliases: None
DOB: N/A
Nationality: Moroccan
Active Years: 2000s
Victims: 6 confirmed
Location: Morocco
MO: Poisoning
Conviction: Sentenced to death

Brief biography:

Adil Albani, a Moroccan serial killer, was convicted of poisoning six people in the 2000s. Albani, whose motives remain unclear, used toxic substances to murder his victims, who were acquaintances or family members. His crimes shocked Morocco and led to a lengthy investigation, resulting in his arrest and conviction. Albani was sentenced to death, although his execution status remains unknown, as Morocco has had a moratorium on executions since the 1990s.

Adolfo Gustavo

Aliases: Adolfo Constanzo
DOB: 1962
Nationality: American
Active Years: 1986-1989
Victims: 15 confirmed
Location: Mexico, USA
MO: Human sacrifice, drug cartel
Conviction: Killed by police in 1989

Brief biography:

Adolfo Constanzo, also known as Adolfo Gustavo, was an American-born cult leader and serial killer who led a drug cartel involved in human sacrifice rituals. Constanzo's cult, which operated out of Mexico in the 1980s, believed that their sacrifices brought them protection and prosperity in their drug operations. His murder spree ended in 1989 when Mexican police closed in on his hideout, and Constanzo ordered one of his followers to kill him to avoid capture. His bizarre and brutal murders have made his story infamous.

Albuquerque Serial Killer

Aliases: West Mesa Bone Collector
DOB: N/A
Nationality: American
Active Years: 2001-2005
Victims: 11 confirmed
Location: New Mexico, USA
MO: Murder and disposal of bodies in desert
Conviction: Unsolved

Brief biography:

The Albuquerque Serial Killer, also known as the West Mesa Bone Collector, is an unidentified serial killer responsible for the deaths of at least 11 women in Albuquerque, New Mexico, between 2001 and 2005. The victims' skeletal remains were discovered in 2009 in a mass grave on the West Mesa, a desolate desert area. Despite intensive investigations and several leads, the killer remains at large, and the case is one of the most notorious unsolved serial murder cases in the United States.

Aida Nourredin Mohammed Abu Zeid

Aliases: Aida Zeid
DOB: 1973
Nationality: Egyptian
Active Years: 1996-1997
Victims: 18 patients murdered
Location: Alexandria, Egypt
MO: Poisoning hospital patients
Conviction: Sentenced to death in 1998, overturned on appeal

Brief biography:

Aida Nourredin Mohammed Abu Zeid was a nurse who confessed to killing 18 hospital patients in Alexandria, Egypt, between 1996 and 1997. She poisoned her victims, and her actions went undetected for some time. Although sentenced to death in 1998, her conviction was later overturned on appeal.

Albert Fentress

Aliases: New York's Own Hannibal Lecter
DOB: 1944
Nationality: American
Active Years: 1979
Victims: 1 confirmed
Location: Poughkeepsie, NY
MO: Lured victim into his home, sexually assaulted, killed, dismembered
Conviction: Found not guilty due to insanity; institutionalized

Brief biography:

Albert Fentress, a high school teacher and meticulous individual, became notorious for his gruesome 1979 murder of a young man named Paul Masters. Known for his eccentric behavior, Fentress meticulously planned the assault, torture, and murder of his victim. A judge declared him insane and he was institutionalized. Despite his recovery and attempts to re-enter society, his case remains infamous, drawing comparisons to Hannibal Lecter.

Aileen Wuornos

Aliases: Lee Blahovec
DOB: February 29, 1956
Nationality: American
Active Years: 1989-1990
Victims: 7 confirmed
Location: Florida
MO: Shot male victims at point-blank range with a .22 caliber handgun
Conviction: Sentenced to death; executed by lethal injection

Brief biography:

Aileen Wuornos, one of the most infamous female serial killers in the U.S., killed seven men between 1989 and 1990. Raised in an abusive and turbulent environment, she turned to prostitution and eventually murder. Wuornos was captured after her lover, Tyria Moore, helped the police secure her confession. Her trial captivated the public, leading to her conviction and eventual execution in 2002.

Albert Fish

Aliases: The Gray Man, The Brooklyn Vampire, The Boogey Man
DOB: May 19, 1870
Nationality: American
Active Years: 1924–1932
Victims: 3 confirmed, suspected of more
Location: New York, USA
MO: Kidnapped, tortured, and cannibalized children
Conviction: Executed by electric chair (1936)

Brief biography:

Albert Fish was an American serial killer and cannibal who preyed on young children. Known for his horrific acts of sadism and cannibalism, Fish was a self-proclaimed masochist who enjoyed inflicting pain on himself and others. He was convicted for the kidnapping and murder of Grace Budd in 1928, a crime for which he sent a letter to the girl's family describing how he had killed and eaten her. Fish claimed to have killed several other children, though only three murders were confirmed. He was executed in 1936 by electric chair at Sing Sing Correctional Facility.

Ali Asghar Borujerdi

Aliases: None
DOB: N/A
Nationality: Iranian
Active Years: 1907-1915
Victims: 33 confirmed
Location: Iran
MO: Poisoning
Conviction: Executed in 1915

Brief biography:

Ali Asghar Borujerdi was an Iranian serial killer active between 1907 and 1915. He was responsible for the deaths of 33 people, mostly through poisoning. Borujerdi used his charm and reputation as a religious healer to gain the trust of his victims before administering lethal doses of poison. His killing spree came to an end when authorities uncovered his crimes. Borujerdi was sentenced to death and executed in 1915. His case remains one of the most infamous in Iranian criminal history.

Ali Baghi

Aliases: None
DOB: N/A
Nationality: Iranian
Active Years: 1980s-1990s
Victims: 9 confirmed
Location: Iran
MO: Strangulation
Conviction: Executed

Brief biography:

Ali Baghi was an Iranian serial killer active during the late 1980s and early 1990s. He targeted vulnerable individuals, especially women, whom he would strangle. His reign of terror gripped the Iranian public until his capture in the early 1990s. Baghi was found guilty of nine murders, although authorities suspect the real number could be higher. He was convicted and sentenced to death, ultimately being executed in the mid-1990s.

Ali Reza Koshruy Kuran (Tehran Vampire)

Aliases: Tehran Vampire
DOB: 1969
Nationality: Iranian
Active Years: 1997
Victims: 9+
Location: Tehran, Iran
MO: Kidnapped, raped, and murdered women; burned bodies
Conviction: Sentenced to death by hanging

Brief biography:

Ali Reza Koshruy Kuran, infamously dubbed the Tehran Vampire, was a serial killer active in Tehran, Iran, in 1997. He preyed on women, kidnapping, raping, and murdering them before setting their bodies on fire to conceal his crimes. Kuran's violent spree lasted for several months, and he was convicted of at least nine murders. Before his execution by hanging on August 12, 1997, in front of a large crowd, he endured public flogging as punishment for his heinous acts. His case remains one of the most gruesome in Iran's criminal history.

Andrew Urdiales

Aliases: None
DOB: June 4, 1964
Nationality: American
Active Years: 1986–1996
Victims: 8
Location: California, Illinois
MO: Shot, raped, and stabbed women in secluded areas
Conviction: Sentenced to death in California, 2018; committed suicide in prison

Brief biography:

Andrew Urdiales, an American serial killer, murdered eight women in California and Illinois between 1986 and 1996. He targeted women in secluded areas, raping and killing them with knives and guns. Urdiales was arrested in 1997 after ballistic tests linked him to several murders. He was convicted and sentenced to death in 2018, but committed suicide in San Quentin State Prison later that year.

Anthrax Killer

Aliases: "Amerithrax"
DOB: Unknown
Nationality: American
Active Years: 2001
Victims: 5 killed, 17 infected
Location: USA
MO: Mailed anthrax-laced letters
Conviction: Unsolved, suspect committed suicide

Brief biography:

The Anthrax Killer, responsible for the 2001 anthrax attacks in the United States, mailed letters containing deadly anthrax spores to media outlets and U.S. senators, killing five people and infecting 17 others. The attacks occurred shortly after the 9/11 terrorist attacks, spreading fear throughout the nation. Dr. Bruce Ivins, a scientist at the U.S. Army Medical Research Institute of Infectious Diseases, was identified as the main suspect but committed suicide in 2008 before he could be formally charged. The case, known as "Amerithrax," remains controversial and officially unsolved.

Anthony Townser

Aliases: N/A
DOB: July 7, 1975
Nationality: American
Active Years: 1993
Victims: 3 confirmed
Location: Illinois and Missouri, USA
MO: Robbery and murder of elderly people
Conviction: 75 years, 1995

Brief biography:

Anthony Townser is a convicted murderer who robbed and killed at least three elderly people in Illinois and Missouri in 1993. His brutal crimes, which shocked local communities, resulted in his conviction and a 75-year prison sentence. He is currently serving his sentence at the Pinckneyville Correctional Center in Illinois.

Anna Margaretha Zwanziger

Aliases: N/A
DOB: August 6, 1760
Nationality: German
Active Years: 1801-1811
Victims: 4+ murdered
Location: Germany
MO: Poisoning her employers
Conviction: Executed by beheading on September 17, 1811

Brief biography:

Anna Margaretha Zwanziger was a German serial killer who poisoned several of her employers with arsenic, including judges she worked for as a housekeeper. She nursed her victims back to health to gain favor, but several of them died. She was convicted of murder and sentenced to death by beheading in 1811.

Alphabet Murders/Double Initial CA

Aliases: None
DOB: N/A
Nationality: American
Active Years: 1970s
Victims: 5 suspected
Location: California, USA
MO: Abduction and strangulation
Conviction: Unsolved

Brief biography:

The Alphabet Murders in California involved the killings of young girls whose first and last initials matched. These murders occurred during the 1970s, and the bodies of the victims were often found in secluded areas. Despite widespread media coverage and intense police investigation, the case remains unsolved. The killer's true identity has never been uncovered, making it one of California's most perplexing serial murder cases.

Alphabet Murders/Double Initial NY

Aliases: None
DOB: N/A
Nationality: American
Active Years: 1970s
Victims: 3 confirmed
Location: New York, USA
MO: Abduction, rape, and strangulation
Conviction: Unsolved

Brief biography:

The Alphabet Murders in New York remain one of the most haunting cold cases in American history. Between 1971 and 1973, three young girls with matching first and last initials were abducted, raped, and strangled. The killer left little evidence, and despite the involvement of the FBI and local law enforcement, no suspect was ever convicted. The case remains unsolved, with many theories but no definitive answers.

Appalachian Trail Murders

Aliases: None
DOB: Various
Nationality: American
Active Years: 1970s-2000s
Victims: 10+
Location: Appalachian Trail, USA
MO: Stabbing, shooting
Conviction: Multiple suspects, varying convictions

Brief biography:

The Appalachian Trail, a popular hiking route in the eastern United States, has been the site of multiple murders over several decades. The most well-known case occurred in 1981 when Robert Mountford Jr. and Laura Ramsay were killed by Randall Lee Smith. Smith served time for the crime but was released in 1996. Several other hikers have been killed or attacked along the trail in later years, leading to increased safety concerns. Some cases remain unsolved, while others have led to arrests and convictions.

Allen Leroy Anderson

Aliases: None
DOB: 1940
Nationality: American
Active Years: 1974-1976
Victims: 5+
Location: Oregon, USA
MO: Strangulation, stabbing
Conviction: Life in prison

Brief biography:

Allen Leroy Anderson, a convicted serial killer from Oregon, was responsible for the murders of at least five people between 1974 and 1976. He primarily targeted young women, strangling and stabbing them before dumping their bodies in remote locations. Anderson was apprehended after forensic evidence linked him to the crime scenes, and he was sentenced to life in prison. His violent spree shocked the Pacific Northwest during the mid-1970s.

Amber Hagerman (Amber Alert System)

Aliases: -
DOB: November 25, 1986
Nationality: American
Active Years: 1996
Victims: 1
Location: Arlington, TX
MO: Abduction, murder
Conviction: Unsolved, no conviction

Brief biography:

Amber Hagerman was abducted and murdered in Arlington, Texas, in January 1996. Her abduction led to the creation of the AMBER Alert system, which notifies the public about child abductions in the hope of a quick recovery. Despite a witness seeing her being abducted, her killer was never caught, and the case remains open.

Amelia Dyer

Aliases: The Ogress of Reading
DOB: 1836
Nationality: British
Active Years: 1860s-1896
Victims: Estimated 300+
Location: England
MO: Strangled infants in her care, disposed of bodies in rivers
Conviction: Sentenced to death; hanged in 1896

Brief biography:

Amelia Dyer, one of the most prolific serial killers in history, operated during the Victorian era in England. Known for her involvement in 'baby farming,' Dyer accepted unwanted infants for money, often killing them soon after. Her gruesome methods of strangling and disposing of children led to the deaths of over 300 infants. After years of evading the law, she was caught and hanged in 1896. Dyer's case caused public outrage, leading to changes in child adoption laws in Britain.

Amelia Sach and Annie Walters

Aliases: Finchley Baby Farmers
DOB: Unknown; Walters: Unknown
Nationality: British
Active Years: Early 1900s
Victims: Estimated 12–20
Location: London, England
MO: Poisoning newborns
Conviction: Both: Executed (1903)

Brief biography:

Amelia Sach and Annie Walters were baby farmers in early 20th century London, where they took in infants under the guise of finding them adoptive families. Instead, they poisoned the babies to dispose of them. They were arrested after police grew suspicious of the high infant mortality rate at their "lying-in" home. Both were convicted and hanged in 1903.

Andrei Chikatilo

Aliases: The Butcher of Rostov
DOB: October 16, 1936
Nationality: Soviet (Russian)
Active Years: 1978–1990
Victims: 52 confirmed
Location: Rostov, Soviet Union (Russia)
MO: Raped, mutilated, and murdered women and children
Conviction: Executed by gunshot (1994)

Brief biography:

Andrei Chikatilo, known as "The Butcher of Rostov," was a Soviet serial killer who terrorized Russia for over a decade. Between 1978 and 1990, Chikatilo sexually assaulted, mutilated, and murdered at least 52 women and children. He often lured his victims from train stations or bus stops, taking them to isolated areas where he would attack them. His brutal murders shocked the Soviet Union and led to one of the largest manhunts in Russian history. Chikatilo was arrested in 1990 and later confessed to his crimes. He was executed by gunshot in 1994.

Amy Wroe Bechtel

Aliases: None
DOB: August 4, 1972
Nationality: American
Active Years: 1997
Victims: 1 (disappeared)
Location: Wind River Mountains, Wyoming, USA
MO: Likely abduction or murder
Conviction: Unsolved; husband Steve Bechtel a suspect but no charges filed

Brief biography:

Amy Wroe Bechtel disappeared on July 24, 1997, after going for a run in the Wind River Mountains of Wyoming. Her car was found abandoned, but no signs of a struggle were apparent. Her husband, Steve Bechtel, became a suspect after journals containing violent content were found, but he has never been charged. The case remains unsolved, and Amy was declared legally dead in 2004.

Amir Qayyam (Brick Killer)

Aliases: Brick Killer
DOB: Unknown
Nationality: Pakistani
Active Years: 2006–2008
Victims: 14
Location: Lahore, Pakistan
MO: Bludgeoning victims with bricks
Conviction: Sentenced to death in 2008

Brief biography:

Amir Qayyam, infamously known as the Brick Killer, was a Pakistani serial killer who murdered 14 people in Lahore between 2006 and 2008. His victims were mainly homeless individuals whom he attacked using bricks. He was convicted and sentenced to death in 2008.

Anatoly Yuriyovych Onoprienko

Aliases: Terminator, Beast of Ukraine
DOB: July 25, 1959
Nationality: Ukrainian
Active Years: 1989–1996
Victims: 52
Location: Ukraine
MO: Shot and burned victims during robberies
Conviction: Sentenced to life imprisonment in 1999

Brief biography:

Anatoly Onoprienko, known as the Terminator or the Beast of Ukraine, was one of Ukraine's most notorious serial killers, responsible for the brutal murders of 52 people between 1989 and 1996. He primarily targeted families during robberies, killing them with a shotgun and burning their homes to eliminate evidence. His killing spree spanned several years, and his cold, calculated murders shocked the nation. Onoprienko was arrested in 1996 and sentenced to life imprisonment in 1999 after confessing to his crimes.

Argarsk Maniac

Aliases: Unknown
DOB: Unknown
Nationality: Russian
Active Years: 2013-2015
Victims: 6+
Location: Argarsk, Russia
MO: Stabbing, bludgeoning
Conviction: Unsolved

Brief biography:

The Argarsk Maniac is an unidentified Russian serial killer who is believed to have murdered at least six people between 2013 and 2015. His victims were primarily young women who were stabbed or bludgeoned to death. Despite numerous investigations and witness reports, the killer remains at large, and his identity is still unknown. The case has left a lasting impact on the small town of Argarsk, where residents live in fear that the killer may strike again.

Arthur Leigh Allen

Aliases: None
DOB: 1933
Nationality: American
Active Years: Suspected 1960s-1970s
Victims: Unknown
Location: California, USA
MO: Suspected Zodiac Killer
Conviction: No conviction

Brief biography:

Arthur Leigh Allen is widely considered a primary suspect in the Zodiac Killer case, one of the most infamous unsolved serial murder cases in American history. Although never convicted, Allen matched several characteristics of the Zodiac, and he was the subject of repeated police investigations throughout the 1970s. Despite mounting circumstantial evidence, including witness descriptions and possible connections to the Zodiac's cryptic letters, Allen died in 1992 without being charged, and the Zodiac Killer's true identity remains a mystery.

Artvin Monster

Aliases: None
DOB: Unknown
Nationality: Turkish
Active Years: 1990s
Victims: 7
Location: Artvin, Turkey
MO: Stabbing, mutilation
Conviction: Executed (before abolishment of death penalty)

Brief biography:

The Artvin Monster was a Turkish serial killer active in the 1990s in the rural province of Artvin. Known for his brutal methods, he targeted women and children, attacking them with knives and leaving their mutilated bodies in remote areas. His reign of terror shocked the small Turkish community until his capture in 1996. After a swift trial, the Artvin Monster was executed, marking one of the last executions in Turkey before the death penalty was abolished.

Arnfinn Nesset

Aliases: None
DOB: 1936
Nationality: Norwegian
Active Years: 1977–1982
Victims: 22
Location: Norway
MO: Poisoning (Curacit)
Conviction: Sentenced to 21 years in prison

Brief biography:

Arnfinn Nesset was a Norwegian nurse and serial killer who murdered at least 22 elderly patients at the Orkdal Nursing Home using a muscle relaxant called Curacit. His killing spree took place over several years before he was caught and convicted in 1983. Nesset was sentenced to 21 years in prison, which was Norway's maximum sentence at the time. He was released in 2004 after serving his full sentence.

Asha Degree

Aliases: None
DOB: August 5, 1990
Nationality: American
Active Years: 2000
Victims: 1 (disappeared)
Location: Shelby, North Carolina, USA
MO: Likely abduction after running away
Conviction: Unsolved; no suspects arrested

Brief biography:

Asha Degree was a 9-year-old girl who disappeared from her Shelby, North Carolina home on February 14, 2000. Witnesses saw her walking along a highway in the early hours of the morning, but she ran into the woods and was never seen again. Despite some of her belongings being found, including a backpack, and numerous investigations, Asha's case remains unsolved, with no solid leads on her fate.

Asghar the Murderer

Aliases: None
DOB: 1890
Nationality: Persian
Active Years: 1920s
Victims: 10+
Location: Persia (Iran)
MO: Stabbing, robbery
Conviction: Executed in 1930
Brief biography:

Asghar the Murderer was a notorious Persian serial killer who terrorized the region of modern-day Iran in the 1920s. Asghar was responsible for the deaths of at least ten people, primarily targeting travelers whom he would rob and murder. His method of operation was brutally simple: he would lure victims into remote areas, stab them to death, and steal their possessions. Asghar was eventually caught by local authorities and executed in 1930, bringing an end to his reign of terror.

Assistant Death in Luzem

Aliases: None
DOB: Unknown
Nationality: Swiss
Active Years: 1990s
Victims: 5+
Location: Lucerne, Switzerland
MO: Assisted suicides, poison
Conviction: Unknown, still under investigation

Brief biography:

The case of the "Assistant Death in Luzem" refers to a string of suspicious deaths in the 1990s in Lucerne, Switzerland, where patients in a hospital were found to have been killed through assisted suicides. The case involved a hospital staff member who facilitated the deaths by providing lethal doses of poison. The investigation revealed ethical and legal challenges in cases involving assisted suicide, and the accused's conviction remains a matter of ongoing investigation. This case drew attention to the complex moral and legal debates surrounding euthanasia in Switzerland.

Ashland Serial Killer

Aliases: None
DOB: Unknown
Nationality: American
Active Years: 1990s
Victims: 5
Location: Ashland, Kentucky

MO: Shooting, strangulation
Conviction: Life in prison

Brief biography:

The Ashland Serial Killer was responsible for the deaths of five people in Ashland, Kentucky, during the 1990s. His crimes involved shooting and strangling his victims, mostly vulnerable individuals such as the homeless. The killer's spree lasted for several years before he was apprehended following a detailed investigation. The case received widespread attention due to the killer's brazen acts of violence in a small, tight-knit community. He was convicted and sentenced to life in prison.

Angel Makers of Nagyrev

Aliases: None
DOB: 1870s-1920s
Nationality: Hungarian
Active Years: 1911-1929
Victims: 50+
Location: Nagyrev, Hungary
MO: Poisoning
Conviction: Multiple life sentences for survivors

Brief biography:
The Angel Makers of Nagyrev were a group of Hungarian women, led by midwife Júlia Fazekas, who poisoned over 50 men in the village of Nagyrev between 1911 and 1929. The women used arsenic to kill their husbands and other male family members, motivated by abuse and desire for freedom. The group was eventually discovered after authorities noticed the suspicious deaths in the village. Several women were arrested and sentenced to life imprisonment, though many were never caught. This case remains one of the most notorious mass poisonings in history.

Anh The Duong

Aliases: None
DOB: 1975
Nationality: Vietnamese-American
Active Years: 1990s
Victims: 9
Location: California, USA
MO: Gunshot, execution-style killings
Conviction: Life in prison

Brief biography:

Anh The Duong was a Vietnamese-American serial killer and gang member who was responsible for a series of execution-style murders in California during the 1990s. Known for his cold-blooded nature, Duong would often target rival gang members and perceived enemies. His violent spree came to an end when he was apprehended in 2003 after a joint investigation between local law enforcement and the FBI. Duong was sentenced to life in prison without the possibility of parole.

Ann Arbor Hospital Murders

Aliases: None
DOB: N/A
Nationality: American
Active Years: 1975
Victims: 10+
Location: Ann Arbor, Michigan
MO: Poisoning, medical malpractice
Conviction: Unsolved

Brief biography:

The Ann Arbor Hospital Murders refer to a string of suspicious deaths at the Veterans Administration Hospital in Ann Arbor, Michigan, in 1975. Several patients died under mysterious circumstances, and it was later discovered that they had been poisoned with a muscle relaxant. Two Filipino nurses were charged in connection with the murders, but the charges were later dropped due to lack of evidence. The case remains unsolved, and the true perpetrator(s) of the murders have never been identified.

Chapter Two: B-List

B1 Butcher

Aliases: None
DOB: Unknown
Nationality: Namibian
Active Years: 2005-2007
Victims: 5
Location: Windhoek, Namibia
MO: Dismemberment, disposal of body parts
Conviction: Unsolved

Brief biography:

The B1 Butcher is the name given to an unidentified serial killer responsible for at least five murders in Namibia between 2005 and 2007. The killer dismembered his victims, disposing of their body parts along Namibia's B1 highway. The gruesome nature of the killings and the methodical way the bodies were disposed of have baffled local authorities, who have yet to apprehend the perpetrator. The case remains unsolved, drawing significant media attention in southern Africa.

Benjamin "Tony" Atkins

Aliases: Woodward Corridor Killer
DOB: August 26, 1968
Nationality: American
Active Years: 1991–1992
Victims: 11 known victims
Location: Detroit, Michigan
MO: Rape, strangulation, dumping bodies in abandoned areas
Conviction: Sentenced to 11 life terms
Brief biography:

Benjamin "Tony" Atkins, known as the Woodward Corridor Killer, was responsible for a string of murders in Detroit, Michigan, between 1991 and 1992. Atkins targeted prostitutes, whom he raped and strangled before disposing of their bodies in abandoned buildings. His reign of terror ended when one of his victims escaped and identified him to the police. Atkins was convicted of 11 murders and sentenced to life in prison without the possibility of parole. He died in 1997 due to complications from HIV while serving his sentence.

Beverley Allitt

Aliases: Angel of Death
DOB: October 4, 1968
Nationality: British
Active Years: February–April 1991
Victims: 4 murdered, 11 attempted
Location: England (Grantham Hospital, Lincolnshire)
MO: Administered lethal doses of insulin and other drugs to children
Conviction: Sentenced to 13 life terms; minimum 30 years, held at Rampton Secure Hospital
Brief biography:

Beverley Allitt, a British nurse dubbed the "Angel of Death," murdered four children and attempted to kill eleven others during her time at Grantham Hospital's children's ward between February and April 1991. Her actions, which involved administering lethal doses of insulin and other drugs, seriously injured six more. Allitt was diagnosed with Munchausen syndrome by proxy, a psychological disorder in which a caregiver inflicts harm to gain attention. Sentenced to life imprisonment, she continues to serve her term at Rampton Secure Hospital. Her case remains one of England's most notorious in the annals of serial crime.

Benjamin "Tony" Atkins

Aliases: None
DOB: 1968
Nationality: American
Active Years: 1991-1992

Victims: 11+
Location: Detroit, Michigan
MO: Strangulation, rape
Conviction: Died in prison (1997)
Brief biography:

Benjamin "Tony" Atkins was an American serial killer active in Detroit, Michigan, during the early 1990s. Known as the "Woodward Corridor Killer," Atkins raped and strangled at least eleven women, many of whom were sex workers or vulnerable individuals. His killing spree spanned less than two years, but the brutality of his crimes shocked the nation. Atkins was arrested in 1992 and sentenced to multiple life sentences. He died in prison of an HIV-related illness in 1997.

Betty Shanks

Aliases: None
DOB: 1931?
Nationality: Australian
Active Years: 1952
Victims: 1
Location: Brisbane, Queensland, Australia
MO: Beaten to death
Conviction: Unsolved
Brief biography:
Betty Shanks was a 22-year-old woman murdered in Brisbane, Australia, in 1952. She was found brutally beaten in a neighbor's garden the day after she failed to return home from university. Despite several suspects and false confessions, no one has ever been arrested for her murder, leaving her case one of Queensland's oldest unsolved mysteries.

Beulah George "Georgia" Tann

Aliases: Georgia Tann
DOB: July 18, 1891
Nationality: American
Active Years: 1924–1950
Victims: 5,000+ (kidnapped children)

Location: Memphis, Tennessee, USA
MO: Kidnapped and sold children, falsified adoption records
Conviction: Died before facing trial; Tennessee Children's Home Society
Brief biography:

Beulah George Tann, infamously known as Georgia Tann, ran the Tennessee Children's Home Society in Memphis, where she orchestrated a black-market baby adoption scheme, kidnapping more than 5,000 children and selling them to wealthy families across the country. Tann exploited poor, single mothers, often stealing their children by telling them the babies had died, and also took children from state wards and mental institutions. Her criminal actions led to a nationwide overhaul of adoption laws. Tann died in 1950 before she could face justice, but her crimes were later exposed, leading to the closure of the Tennessee Children's Home Society.

Bevan Spencer von Einem

Aliases: None
DOB: May 29, 1946
Nationality: Australian
Active Years: 1979–1983
Victims: 1 confirmed (suspected of 5+ more)
Location: Adelaide, Australia
MO: Kidnapped, tortured, and murdered young boys
Conviction: Serving life imprisonment in Yatala Prison
Brief biography:
Bevan Spencer von Einem was convicted of the murder of 15-year-old Richard Kelvin, whom he kidnapped, tortured, and murdered in Adelaide, Australia in 1983. He held Kelvin captive for several weeks before his death. Von Einem is also suspected of being involved in the unsolved "Family Murders," which include the killings of five other young men in Adelaide between 1979 and 1983. He remains in prison, serving a life sentence.

Billy Ray Waldon

Aliases: Billy Joe Waldon
DOB: January 3, 1952
Nationality: American

Active Years: 1985
Victims: 4
Location: Oklahoma and California, USA
MO: Thrill-killed, shot victims
Conviction: Sentenced to death, San Quentin Prison
Brief biography:
Billy Ray Waldon, a thrill-killer active in 1985, murdered four people in Oklahoma and California. His killing spree was short-lived but brutal, involving shootings and robberies. He was placed on the FBI's "Ten Most Wanted" list in May 1986 and captured two months later. Waldon was convicted in 1987 and is currently on death row in San Quentin State Prison. Interestingly, Waldon is also the creator of a constructed language known as "Poliespo."

Bobby Dunbar

Aliases: None
DOB: 1908
Nationality: American
Active Years: 1912
Victims: 1 (disappeared)
Location: Opelousas, Louisiana, USA
MO: Child abduction and wrongful identification
Conviction: Solved in 2004 via DNA testing confirming Bobby was not found
Brief biography:

Bobby Dunbar disappeared in 1912 at the age of 4 while on a fishing trip. After an extensive search, a boy believed to be Bobby was found with a man named William Walters. However, a woman claimed the boy was her son, Bruce Anderson. A court awarded custody to the Dunbars. In 2004, DNA testing proved the boy was not Bobby Dunbar, leaving the mystery of what happened to Bobby unresolved.

Bobbie Sue Terrell

Aliases: None
DOB: October 16, 1952
Nationality: American

Active Years: 1980–1986
Victims: 12 confirmed
Location: Florida, Illinois
MO: Insulin overdose on elderly patients
Conviction: 65 years in prison, died 2007
Brief biography:

Bobbie Sue Terrell was a nurse diagnosed with schizophrenia and Munchausen syndrome by proxy. She killed 12 elderly patients in St. Petersburg, Florida, using insulin overdoses, all while calling the police and mutilating herself to deflect suspicion. Terrell's actions came to light when her psychiatric history was uncovered. In 1986, she was sentenced to 65 years in prison and died in 2007 while serving her term.

Boone Helm

Aliases: The Kentucky Cannibal
DOB: January 28, 1828
Nationality: American
Active Years: 1850s–1860s
Victims: Estimated 11+
Location: Western U.S. (California, Idaho, Montana)
MO: Cannibalism, murder by stabbing and shooting
Conviction: Executed by hanging, 1864
Brief biography:
Boone Helm, notorious as the "Kentucky Cannibal," was an American serial killer and cannibal who roamed the Western U.S. during the mid-1800s. Known for his violent tendencies, Helm killed and ate many of his victims, often during treacherous journeys through the wilderness. He gained infamy for killing his traveling companions and resorting to cannibalism for survival. Helm joined a gang of robbers and murderers, leading to his capture and execution by hanging in 1864 in Virginia City, Montana. His life of brutality and cannibalism has made him a gruesome figure in the annals of frontier history.

Bogdan Eugeniusz Arnold

Aliases: None
DOB: 1933
Nationality: Polish
Active Years: 1966-1967
Victims: 4
Location: Katowice, Poland
MO: Strangulation, decapitation
Conviction: Executed in 1968
Brief biography:

Bogdan Eugeniusz Arnold was a Polish serial killer who murdered four women in the city of Katowice between 1966 and 1967. Arnold, who struggled with relationships, lured women to his apartment before strangling them and decapitating their bodies. His gruesome crimes were discovered when neighbors complained of a foul odor emanating from his apartment. Arnold was arrested, tried, and sentenced to death. He was executed in 1968, leaving behind a legacy as one of Poland's most chilling murderers.

Brandon Tholmer

Aliases: None
DOB: 1949
Nationality: American
Active Years: 1981–1984
Victims: 34 suspected rapes/murders
Location: Los Angeles, California
MO: Raped, robbed, and murdered elderly women
Conviction: 4 life sentences, 1986
Brief biography:

Brandon Tholmer was born in New Orleans, Louisiana, and is suspected of raping and murdering 34 elderly women in Los Angeles between 1981 and 1984. Tholmer's crimes targeted vulnerable elderly women, and his spree ended with his arrest in 1984. He was sentenced to four consecutive life terms in 1986 and remains incarcerated at the California Medical Facility.

Bruce Mendenhall

Aliases: Truck Stop Killer
DOB: April 14, 1951
Nationality: American
Active Years: 1992–2007
Victims: 5 confirmed (suspected 9)
Location: Multiple states, USA
MO: Shooting, strangulation, abduction
Conviction: Life imprisonment, 2007
Brief biography:

Bruce Mendenhall, a long-haul truck driver, is a convicted serial killer known as the Truck Stop Killer. He preyed on women at truck stops across several U.S. states, murdering at least five confirmed victims. His violent spree involved shooting, strangulation, and other brutal methods. Mendenhall was arrested in 2007 after DNA evidence linked him to multiple murders, and he is suspected of having committed at least nine murders. He is serving a life sentence in prison.

Chapter Three: C-List

Carl Panzram

Aliases: None known
DOB: June 28, 1891
Nationality: American
Active Years: 1920–1929
Victims: Claimed 21+
Location: United States
MO: Lured, raped, and murdered victims, often disposing of bodies in rivers
Conviction: Executed by hanging in 1930
Brief biography:

Carl Panzram, one of the most remorseless serial killers in American history, claimed to have killed 21 people and committed numerous other crimes, including sodomy and burglary. Known for his deep hatred of humanity, Panzram's violent spree began in 1920. His killing methods included luring victims, especially sailors, and murdering them after robbing and raping them. Panzram was arrested in 1928 and later sentenced to death for killing a prison foreman. He was executed in 1930 without ever showing remorse for his crimes.

Cary Stayner

Aliases: Yosemite Park Killer
DOB: August 13, 1961
Nationality: American
Active Years: 1999
Victims: 4 murdered
Location: Yosemite National Park, USA
MO: Strangled, decapitated, mutilated victims
Conviction: Sentenced to death in 2002, on death row at San Quentin Penitentiary
Brief biography:

Cary Stayner, the "Yosemite Park Killer," committed four brutal murders in 1999 in and around Yosemite National Park. His victims included Carole Sund, her daughter Juli, Silvina Pelosso, and Joie Ruth Armstrong. Stayner was arrested after confessing to the murders, and despite pleading not guilty by reason of insanity, he was convicted and sentenced to death in 2002. He remains on death row at San Quentin Penitentiary.

Charles Albanese

Aliases: None
DOB: 1937
Nationality: American
Active Years: 1980-1981
Victims: 3 confirmed
Location: Illinois, USA
MO: Poisoning (arsenic)
Conviction: Executed in 1995
Brief biography:

Charles Albanese was an American businessman turned serial killer who poisoned three family members using arsenic in the early 1980s. Motivated by financial gain, Albanese sought to inherit his victims' estates. He carefully planned the murders to appear as natural deaths but was eventually caught when traces of arsenic were found in the victims' bodies during autopsies. Albanese was convicted and sentenced to death in 1982. He was executed in 1995 by lethal injection.

Charles Frederick Albright

Aliases: The Eyeball Killer
DOB: 1933
Nationality: American
Active Years: 1990-1991
Victims: 3 confirmed
Location: Texas, USA
MO: Shot prostitutes, removed their eyes
Conviction: Life imprisonment
Brief biography:

Charles Frederick Albright, also known as the Eyeball Killer, was a Texan serial killer who gained notoriety for his gruesome signature of removing his victims' eyes. Between 1990 and 1991, Albright targeted prostitutes, shooting them before meticulously removing their eyes with surgical precision. Despite the grotesque nature of his crimes, Albright managed to evade capture for several months. He was eventually caught through forensic evidence and sentenced to life in prison without parole.

Charles Kwabeno Ebo Quansah

Aliases: Accra Strangler
DOB: 1964
Nationality: Ghanaian
Active Years: 1990s–2001
Victims: 9 (suspected of 34)
Location: Accra, Ghana
MO: Strangling female victims
Conviction: Sentenced to death in 2003
Brief biography:

The Accra Strangler is an unidentified serial killer responsible for the deaths of 34 women in Accra, Ghana, in 2009. The killer's victims were predominantly young women, and all were strangled in various hotels around the capital city. Despite extensive investigations, including media campaigns and public appeals, the case remains unsolved. The murders led to widespread fear in the city, and the killer's identity remains a mystery.

Charles Manson

Aliases: None
DOB: November 12, 1934
Nationality: American
Active Years: 1960s–1970
Victims: 8 direct murders (via cult)
Location: Los Angeles, California
MO: Cult leader, manipulation, ordering murders
Conviction: Life imprisonment (commuted from death)
Brief biography:

Charles Manson, the notorious cult leader, gained infamy for orchestrating a series of brutal murders in Los Angeles during the late 1960s without physically committing them himself. His followers, known as "The Manson Family," were responsible for the high-profile murders of actress Sharon Tate and several others.

Manson's delusional belief in an apocalyptic race war called "Helter Skelter," fueled by drugs, led him to manipulate his followers into carrying out his murderous plans. Sentenced to death in 1971, his sentence was later commuted to life imprisonment. Manson remained a chilling symbol of manipulation and violence until his death in 2017.

Charles Ng

Aliases: None
DOB: December 24, 1960
Nationality: Hong Kong (Chinese-American)
Active Years: 1983–1985
Victims: 11+ (suspected of more)
Location: United States
MO: Kidnapping, torture, murder
Conviction: Sentenced to death, 1999
Brief biography:

Charles Ng, along with his accomplice Leonard Lake, kidnapped, tortured, and killed at least 11 people during the early 1980s. Operating out of a ranch in California, the pair's "operation" was designed to create a survivalist bunker where women would be kept as sex slaves. Lake committed suicide after being apprehended by the police, but Ng fled to Canada and was only extradited after a lengthy legal battle. Ng was convicted of 11 murders in 1999 and sentenced to death, where he remains on death row.

Chaim Weiss

Aliases: None
DOB: 1970
Nationality: American
Active Years: 1986
Victims: 1 (Chaim Weiss)
Location: Torah High School, New York
MO: Bludgeoned to death in his dormitory
Conviction: Unsolved

Brief biography:

Chaim Weiss was a 15-year-old student at Torah High School in New York, where he was murdered in his dorm room in 1986. He was struck in the head twice with a hatchet-like weapon. Strange elements, such as an open window on a cold night and his body being moved post-mortem, have baffled investigators for decades. Despite suspicions that someone within the religious community may know more, no arrests have been made, and his murder remains a mystery.

Chester DeWayne Turner

Aliases: None
DOB: November 5, 1966
Nationality: American
Active Years: 1987–1998
Victims: 13 confirmed
Location: Los Angeles, California
MO: Strangulation, rape
Conviction: Death sentence, 2007
Brief biography:

Chester DeWayne Turner is an American serial killer responsible for the deaths of at least 13 women between 1987 and 1998. His victims were primarily women involved in prostitution in the Los Angeles area. Turner's preferred method of killing was strangulation, often followed by sexual assault. DNA evidence eventually linked him to the murders, and in 2007, he was sentenced to death for his crimes. He is currently on death row in San Quentin State Prison.

Christopher Bernard Wilder

Aliases: None
DOB: March 13, 1945
Nationality: Australian-American
Active Years: 1984
Victims: 8+ known victims
Location: Multiple U.S. states
MO: Kidnapping, sexual assault, murder, mutilation
Conviction: Died in a shootout with police in 1984
Brief biography:

Christopher Bernard Wilder, an Australian-born serial killer and rapist, terrorized the United States in 1984. He lured young women with promises of modeling opportunities before sexually assaulting and murdering them. Wilder's crimes spanned several states, and he was involved in the deaths of at least eight women during his cross-country killing spree. His horrifying acts of violence included torture and mutilation. Wilder was eventually cornered by police in New Hampshire, where he died during a shootout in April 1984. His killing spree shocked the nation and has been the subject of numerous true crime documentaries.

Christopher Robin Worrell & James William Miller (Truro Murders)

Aliases: None
DOB: Christopher Worrell - 1954, James William Miller - 1940
Nationality: Australian
Active Years: 1976–1977
Victims: 7 confirmed
Location: South Australia
MO: Abduction, strangulation
Conviction: Worrell died in car crash; Miller sentenced to life
Brief biography:

Christopher Worrell and James William Miller were responsible for the infamous Truro Murders in South Australia, during which they abducted, raped, and murdered seven women. Worrell was the dominant partner in the relationship, while Miller facilitated the abductions and served as his accomplice. The murders took place between 1976 and 1977, and the bodies were discovered in 1979. Worrell died in a car crash in 1977, and Miller was later convicted of six of the murders, receiving a life sentence. He died in prison in 2008.

Clarence Walker

Aliases: None
DOB: February 25, 1929
Nationality: American
Active Years: 1945–1966
Victims: At least 14
Location: Tennessee, Ohio, Michigan, USA
MO: Murdered women, children, and a boy

Conviction: Sentenced to 320 years in Illinois
Brief biography:

Clarence Walker is suspected of murdering at least 14 people, including women, children, and a teenage boy, across Tennessee, Ohio, and Michigan between 1945 and 1966. His reign of terror was punctuated by violent sexual assaults. Walker was first sentenced to seven years for manslaughter in 1945, but his most severe sentence came in 1968 when he was handed 320 years for attempted murder, rape, and robbery in Illinois.

Cleveland Torso Murderer

Aliases: Cleveland Torso Murderer
DOB: Unknown
Nationality: American
Active Years: 1935–1938
Victims: 12
Location: Cleveland, Ohio
MO: Dismembered victims, left torsos scattered
Conviction: Unsolved case, no conviction
Brief biography:

The Cleveland Torso Murderer terrorized the city of Cleveland during the 1930s, killing at least 12 victims, most of them vagrants. The killer dismembered the bodies, often leaving the headless torsos in the poor Kingsbury Run neighborhood. Despite police efforts, including those of famed detective Eliot Ness, the killer was never identified. The case remains one of the most disturbing unsolved mysteries in American history.

Corey Hamlet

Aliases: None
DOB: Unknown
Nationality: American
Active Years: 2010–2014
Victims: Multiple (exact number unknown)
Location: Newark, New Jersey
MO: Gang leader, racketeering, ordering murders

Conviction: Life imprisonment (two concurrent terms)
Brief biography:

Corey Hamlet, the ruthless leader of the Grape Street Crips in Newark, New Jersey, was known for orchestrating a wave of violence, murder, and drug trafficking in the city from 2010 to 2014. Under his leadership, the gang operated like a criminal enterprise, dealing in illegal drugs and using extreme violence to maintain control of the streets. Hamlet personally ordered murders and engaged in racketeering to assert his dominance, leaving Newark in a state of fear. His activities came to an end after a comprehensive federal investigation led to his arrest. In 2016, Hamlet was convicted of multiple charges, including murder and racketeering, and sentenced to life imprisonment.

Curtis Dean Anderson

Aliases: None
DOB: 1968
Nationality: American
Active Years: 1997-2000
Victims: 4+
Location: California, USA
MO: Abduction, sexual assault, strangulation
Conviction: Died in prison
Brief biography:

Curtis Dean Anderson was a serial killer and child molester who abducted, sexually assaulted, and killed young girls in California between 1997 and 2000. His known victims included Xiana Fairchild, an 8-year-old whose disappearance led to a nationwide search. Anderson was apprehended in 2000 and convicted of multiple murders. He died in prison in 2007 from natural causes before he could be tried for all of his suspected crimes.

Chapter Four: D-List

Dale Anderson

Aliases: None
DOB: 1952
Nationality: American
Active Years: 1980-1981
Victims: 3
Location: Oklahoma, USA
MO: Stabbing, bludgeoning
Conviction: Life in prison
Brief biography:

Dale Anderson was an American serial killer who murdered three people in Oklahoma during the early 1980s. Anderson's victims were all acquaintances whom he brutally attacked with knives or blunt objects. Known for his violent temper, Anderson was quickly apprehended after the discovery of his third victim. He was sentenced to life in prison without the possibility of parole.

Danny Bible

Aliases: Acres Homes Killer
DOB: 1957
Nationality: American
Active Years: 1980s
Victims: 4 confirmed
Location: Texas, USA
MO: Raped and murdered women
Conviction: Executed in 2018
Brief biography:

Danny Bible, also known as the Acres Homes Killer, was a Texas serial killer and rapist who murdered four women in the 1980s. Bible's first victim was a young woman whom he raped and stabbed in 1979, and he went on to kill several more women. After being on the run for years, Bible was captured in the late 1990s and sentenced to death. He was executed by lethal injection in 2018. Bible's gruesome crimes earned him a place among Texas' most notorious killers.

Darren Deon Vann

Aliases: None
DOB: March 21, 1971
Nationality: American
Active Years: 2009-2014
Victims: 7 confirmed
Location: Indiana, USA
MO: Strangulation, sexual assault
Conviction: Life imprisonment, charged in 2016
Brief biography:

Darren Deon Vann, an American serial killer, targeted women, many of whom were involved in prostitution. His killing spree, uncovered in 2014, included seven victims, though he claimed more. Vann lured his victims to motels, where he strangled them. His arrest followed the discovery of Afrikka Hardy's body, which led to the uncovering of six more bodies. Vann was charged with multiple murders and sentenced to life imprisonment.

David Berkowitz

Aliases: Son of Sam
DOB: June 1, 1953
Nationality: American
Active Years: 1976–1977
Victims: 6 confirmed
Location: New York City, USA
MO: Shot victims with a .44 caliber revolver
Conviction: Life imprisonment (1978)
Brief biography:

David Berkowitz, known as the "Son of Sam," terrorized New York City during the summer of 1976 and 1977, shooting six people to death and wounding several others in a series of random attacks. Berkowitz taunted the police with letters, signing them with the name "Son of Sam." His crimes created a media frenzy and widespread panic in the city. He was eventually caught after a parking ticket led police to his car. Berkowitz claimed that a demonic dog named Sam told him to commit the murders. He was sentenced to life imprisonment in 1978, where he remains today, having since become a born-again Christian.

David and Catherine Birnie

Aliases: None
DOB: David: February 16, 1951; Catherine: May 23, 1951
Nationality: Australian
Active Years: 1986
Victims: 4 confirmed
Location: Perth, Western Australia
MO: Kidnapping, rape, and murder
Conviction: Both sentenced to life in prison; David committed suicide in 2005
Brief biography:

David and Catherine Birnie, an Australian couple known for their gruesome series of rapes and murders, lured women into their home, where David would repeatedly rape them while Catherine watched. Their spree ended when their final intended victim, Kate Moir, escaped and contacted police. The couple was convicted of four murders, and David later killed himself in prison. Catherine remains incarcerated, becoming only the second woman in Australian history to receive a "never to be released" life sentence.

David Joseph Carpenter

Aliases: Trailside Killer
DOB: May 6, 1930
Nationality: American
Active Years: 1979–1981
Victims: 10 confirmed
Location: California, USA
MO: Shooting, stabbing, sexual assault
Conviction: Death sentence (twice), 1984 and 1988
Brief biography:

David Joseph Carpenter, known as the Trailside Killer, terrorized hiking trails in California's state parks from 1979 to 1981. He raped, shot, and stabbed at least 10 people, most of whom were women. Carpenter's criminal career began in his youth, and his violent tendencies escalated over time. After a series of murders, he was finally arrested in 1981 and convicted of multiple murders. He was sentenced to death twice, once in 1984 and again in 1988, and remains on death row at San Quentin State Prison.

Darya Nikolayevna Saltykova

Aliases: Saltychikha
DOB: March 11, 1730
Nationality: Russian
Active Years: 1756-1762
Victims: 38+
Location: Russia
MO: Tortured and murdered servants
Conviction: Life imprisonment in a convent
Brief biography:

Darya Nikolayevna Saltykova was a Russian noblewoman who tortured and killed over 100 of her servants, mainly young women. After years of complaints, Empress Catherine II ordered an investigation, and Darya was convicted of 38 murders. Due to the abolition of the death penalty in Russia, she was publicly shamed and then imprisoned for life in a convent.

Dean Corll

Aliases: The Candy Man
DOB: December 24, 1939
Nationality: American
Active Years: 1970–1973
Victims: 28+
Location: Texas, USA
MO: Torture, sexual assault, murder
Conviction: Killed by accomplice in 1973
Brief biography:

Dean Corll, also known as "The Candy Man," was an American serial killer who, with the help of two teenage accomplices, murdered at least 28 young boys between 1970 and 1973. Corll lured his victims with promises of candy, raped, tortured, and killed them in his home. His killing spree ended when one of his accomplices, Elmer

Wayne Henley, shot and killed him during an attempted murder. Henley later confessed to his involvement and was sentenced to six consecutive 99-year terms.

Dennis Rader

Aliases: BTK Killer
DOB: March 9, 1945
Nationality: American
Active Years: 1974–1991
Victims: 10
Location: Wichita, Kansas, USA
MO: Bind, torture, and kill victims, mostly women
Conviction: Convicted of 10 murders; sentenced to life in prison
Brief biography:

Dennis Rader, known as the BTK Killer (an acronym for "Bind, Torture, Kill"), was a seemingly ordinary man who terrorized Wichita, Kansas, for decades. Rader's reign of terror began in 1974, targeting mostly women, and his methods involved binding, torturing, and killing his victims. Despite his active participation in the local church and as a Boy Scout leader, Rader hid his sadistic tendencies from those around him. His killing spree abruptly ended in 1991, but he resurfaced in 2004, taunting police with letters. This ultimately led to his arrest in 2005. In 2005, he was sentenced to 10 consecutive life terms for the murders of 10 people. His calculated cruelty and ability to live a double life shocked the world.

Dennis Nilsen

Aliases: The Muswell Hill Murderer
DOB: November 23, 1945
Nationality: British
Active Years: 1978–1983
Victims: 15 confirmed
Location: London, England
MO: Strangled and drowned men, kept bodies
Conviction: Life imprisonment (1983), died in 2018
Brief biography:

Dennis Nilsen, also known as "The Muswell Hill Murderer," was a British serial killer who killed at least 15 young men between 1978 and 1983. Nilsen would lure his victims, usually homeless men or drifters, to his home, where he would strangle and drown them before keeping their bodies for extended periods. He often engaged in necrophilia with the corpses before dismembering them. Nilsen was caught after human remains clogged the drains of his apartment building. He was sentenced to life imprisonment and died in prison in 2018.

Debra Brown and Alton Coleman

Aliases: None
DOB: Brown: November 11, 1962; Coleman: November 6, 1955
Nationality: American
Active Years: 1984
Victims: 7 confirmed
Location: Midwest U.S.
MO: Kidnapping, rape, and murder of adults and children
Conviction: Coleman executed in 2002; Brown's death sentence commuted to life imprisonment
Brief biography:

Debra Brown and Alton Coleman embarked on a killing spree across the Midwest in 1984, committing seven murders and numerous rapes and robberies. The couple used their relationship to lure children and young women into their traps, often befriending them before attacking. While Coleman was executed in 2002, Debra Brown's death sentence was commuted to life imprisonment due to her low IQ and dependent personality.

Diogo Alves

Aliases: None
DOB: 1810
Nationality: Portuguese
Active Years: 1836-1840
Victims: 70+ suspected
Location: Lisbon, Portugal
MO: Robbery, drowning victims
Conviction: Executed
Brief biography:

Diogo Alves was a notorious Portuguese serial killer active in the 19th century. Between 1836 and 1840, Alves is suspected of robbing and killing over 70 people, primarily by throwing them off the Aqueduto das Águas Livres in Lisbon. His reign of terror ended in 1840 when he was arrested and subsequently hanged. Alves's preserved head remains a macabre artifact in a Lisbon medical school, adding a chilling legacy to his story.

Dimitris Vakrinos

Aliases: None
DOB: 1962
Nationality: Greek
Active Years: 1987–1997
Victims: 7 confirmed, suspected more
Location: Greece
MO: Shot and burned victims
Conviction: Committed suicide in prison, 1997
Brief biography:

Dimitris Vakrinos was a Greek serial killer and taxi driver who killed seven people between 1987 and 1997. He used a variety of methods, including shooting and burning his victims alive. Vakrinos targeted rivals, acquaintances, and strangers. After his arrest in 1997, he was found guilty of multiple murders and sentenced to life imprisonment. He committed suicide in prison shortly after his conviction.

Dorothy Arnold

Aliases: None
DOB: July 1, 1885
Nationality: American
Active Years: 1910
Victims: 1 (disappeared)
Location: New York City, USA
MO: Disappearance after shopping
Conviction: Unsolved; no suspects or body found
Brief biography:

Dorothy Arnold, a wealthy New York socialite, disappeared on December 12, 1910, while shopping in Manhattan. Despite exhaustive searches and private investigations by her family, no trace of Dorothy was ever found. Various theories emerged, including her running away or being abducted, but no evidence has surfaced to confirm what happened to her. The case remains one of New York's most famous unsolved disappearances.

Dorothy Jane Scott

Aliases: None
DOB: 1948
Nationality: American
Active Years: 1980
Victims: 1 (Dorothy Scott)
Location: Santa Ana, California
MO: Stalked and murdered, car found abandoned
Conviction: Unsolved
Brief biography:

Dorothy Jane Scott was a single mother who began receiving harassing phone calls in early 1980. On May 28, 1980, after helping a coworker to the hospital, Dorothy disappeared. Her car was found burning in an alley, but her body wasn't found until four years later, when her remains were discovered with dog bones in a remote area. Her stalker continued to torment her family for years with phone calls claiming responsibility for her death, but he was never identified, and her murder remains unsolved.

Dr. Thomas Lars Allgen

Aliases: None
DOB: 1932
Nationality: Swedish
Active Years: 1960s-1970s
Victims: 3 confirmed
Location: Sweden
MO: Poisoning
Conviction: Sentenced to life
Brief biography:

Dr. Thomas Lars Allgen, a Swedish physician, was convicted of poisoning three patients during the 1960s and 1970s. His crimes involved administering lethal doses of medication to his victims, who were under his care at the time. Despite his respected position in the medical community, Allgen's actions were eventually uncovered, and he was sentenced to life imprisonment in Sweden. His case became notorious for highlighting the vulnerability of patients under medical authority.

Donald Neilson

Aliases: Nappy, Black Panther
DOB: 1936
Nationality: British
Active Years: 1974–1975
Victims: 4
Location: England
MO: Kidnapping, shooting
Conviction: Life imprisonment
Brief biography:

Donald Neilson, known as the "Black Panther" and later "Nappy," was a British serial killer and armed robber. He kidnapped and killed four people during the 1970s, most notably a young heiress named Lesley Whittle, whom he held for ransom before murdering her. Neilson was sentenced to life in prison and died in 2011 while serving his sentence.

Chapter Five: E-List

Earle Leonard Nelson

Aliases: Gorilla Killer
DOB: 1897
Nationality: American
Active Years: 1926–1927
Victims: 22
Location: USA, Canada
MO: Strangulation
Conviction: Executed in 1928
Brief biography:

Earle Leonard Nelson, also known as the "Gorilla Killer," was an American-Canadian serial killer who murdered 22 women during the 1920s. He would strangle his victims and leave their bodies in grotesque positions. Nelson was eventually captured in Canada and extradited to the U.S., where he was convicted and executed by hanging in 1928.

Ed Gein

Aliases: The Plainfield Ghoul, The Butcher of Plainfield
DOB: August 27, 1906
Nationality: American
Active Years: 1947–1957
Victims: 2 confirmed, others suspected
Location: Plainfield, Wisconsin, USA
MO: Murder, grave-robbing, making items from human remains
Conviction: Found guilty but legally insane, committed to a mental institution
Brief biography:

Ed Gein became infamous for his gruesome activities in Plainfield, Wisconsin. He was a grave-robber who made objects from human body parts, including a belt made of nipples and lampshades from human skin. Gein also murdered two women: Bernice Worden and Mary Hogan. His disturbing acts inspired fictional characters like Norman Bates and Leatherface. Declared insane, Gein was committed to a mental health facility until his death.

Edmund Kemper

Aliases: The Co-ed Killer
DOB: December 18, 1948
Nationality: American
Active Years: 1964, 1972–1973
Victims: 10 confirmed
Location: California
MO: Murdered women, including his mother, raped and dismembered bodies
Conviction: Sentenced to life imprisonment, 1973
Brief biography:

Edmund Kemper, the "Co-ed Killer," was a serial killer active in California during the early 1970s. His spree began at age 15 when he killed his grandparents. After release from a psychiatric hospital, Kemper murdered eight young women and his mother, mutilating and raping the bodies before disposing of them. He eventually turned himself in and, though requesting the death penalty, was sentenced to life imprisonment in 1973.

Edgar Ernesto Alvarez Cruz

Aliases: None
DOB: 1970
Nationality: Salvadoran
Active Years: 1990s-2000s
Victims: 5 confirmed
Location: El Salvador
MO: Torture and murder
Conviction: Sentenced to death
Brief biography:

Edgar Ernesto Alvarez Cruz was a Salvadoran serial killer known for torturing his victims before killing them. His brutal methods shocked the public, and he was convicted of five murders, though authorities believe the true number may be higher. His crimes were part of a larger wave of violence in El Salvador during the 1990s and early 2000s. Alvarez Cruz was sentenced to death.

Edward L. Tenney

Aliases: None
DOB: July 30, 1959
Nationality: American
Active Years: 1993
Victims: 3
Location: Aurora, Illinois, USA
MO: Shot victims during home robberies
Conviction: Sentenced to death
Brief biography:

Edward L. Tenney was an American serial killer responsible for three murders in Aurora, Illinois, in 1993. He shot his victims during home robberies, showing a shocking disregard for human life. His crimes included killing a man for only $6. Tenney was convicted of these murders and sentenced to death, though Illinois later abolished the death penalty. His cold-blooded killings left a lasting impact on the local community.

Edward Walton

Aliases: None
DOB: 1870s
Nationality: American
Active Years: 1896–1908
Victims: 5
Location: Alabama, Illinois, Ohio, West Virginia, USA
MO: Shot, robbed, and beat victims
Conviction: Executed in 1908
Brief biography:

Edward Walton confessed to five murders across multiple states from 1896 to 1908, involving robbery and brutal beatings. Captured after a standoff with police in 1908, he confessed to his crimes and was executed by hanging on July 17, 1908.

Elizabeth Bathory

Aliases: The Blood Countess
DOB: August 7, 1560

Nationality: Hungarian
Active Years: 1585–1610
Victims: Estimated 600+
Location: Hungary
MO: Tortured and murdered young women, allegedly bathing in their blood
Conviction: Confined to castle, died in 1614
Brief biography:

Elizabeth Bathory, the "Blood Countess," was a Hungarian noblewoman accused of torturing and killing hundreds of young women. Legends suggest she bathed in their blood to preserve her youth. Her noble status shielded her until she targeted young noblewomen. Bathory was never formally tried but was confined to her castle, where she died in 1614.

Elizabeth Short

Aliases: The Black Dahlia
DOB: July 29, 1924
Nationality: American
Active Years: 1947
Victims: 1
Location: Los Angeles, CA
MO: Mutilation, body bisected, drained of blood
Conviction: Never solved, no conviction
Brief biography:

Elizabeth Short, famously known as the Black Dahlia, was found murdered in Los Angeles in 1947, with her body bisected and posed in a vacant lot. The extreme mutilation and lack of blood at the scene shocked the nation. Despite numerous suspects, the case remains unsolved, becoming one of the most infamous cold cases in American history.

Elizabeth van Valkenburgh

Aliases: None
DOB: July 1799
Nationality: American
Active Years: 1833-1846
Victims: 2 confirmed (husbands)

Location: New York, USA
MO: Poisoning with arsenic
Conviction: Sentenced to death, hanged in 1846
Brief biography:

Elizabeth van Valkenburgh poisoned her two husbands with arsenic. Known for her abusive relationships, she sought control over her alcoholic spouses. After the death of her second husband, she was arrested and sentenced to death. Due to her obesity and a broken leg, she was carried to the gallows in a rocking chair and hanged in 1846.

Elizabeth Woolcock

Aliases: Adelaide Child
DOB: 1848
Nationality: Australian
Active Years: 1870
Victims: 1 confirmed
Location: South Australia
MO: Poisoned her husband
Conviction: Executed in 1873
Brief biography:

Elizabeth Woolcock, known as the Adelaide Child, was convicted of poisoning her husband in 1870. Her case became infamous due to the gruesome nature of her crime and subsequent trial. Woolcock was found guilty and sentenced to death, becoming the only woman executed in South Australia. Her case remains significant in Australian criminal history, sparking debates about her trial's fairness.

Elias Abuelazam

Aliases: The Flint Serial Stabber
DOB: 1976
Nationality: Israeli
Active Years: 2009-2010
Victims: 5 confirmed, 18 injured

Location: Michigan, USA; Virginia, USA
MO: Stabbed random victims
Conviction: Sentenced to life
Brief biography:

Elias Abuelazam is an Israeli-American serial killer who embarked on a violent stabbing spree across several U.S. states between 2009 and 2010. His attacks appeared random, targeting mostly African American men, whom he stabbed in public spaces. Abuelazam was arrested in 2010 while trying to flee the country. He was convicted of multiple murders and sentenced to life in prison. His case brought national attention due to the randomness of his attacks and the racial undertones of his crime spree.

Chapter Six: F-List

Felicitas Aguillon

Aliases: None
DOB: Unknown
Nationality: Filipino
Active Years: 1980s-1990s
Victims: 6 confirmed
Location: Philippines
MO: Poisoning
Conviction: Sentenced to life

Brief biography:

Felicitas Aguillon was a Filipino serial killer who poisoned six of her neighbors and acquaintances over the course of the 1980s and 1990s. Aguillon's motives were believed to be financial, as she often befriended her victims before poisoning them to take over their assets. She was eventually caught and sentenced to life in prison. Her case remains one of the most notorious serial murder cases in the Philippines.

Felícitas Sánchez Aguillón

Aliases: The Ogress of Colonia Roma
DOB: 1890
Nationality: Mexican
Active Years: 1930s
Victims: Estimated 50+
Location: Mexico City
MO: Baby farming, infanticide
Conviction: Arrested, committed suicide before trial
Brief biography:

Felícitas Sánchez Aguillón, known as the "Ogress of Colonia Roma," was a Mexican nurse and midwife who murdered infants and children during the 1930s. She operated a baby farming business, where she would kill unwanted children, disposing of their bodies in sewers or incinerators. Arrested after remains were found near her home, she committed suicide three months later.

Flannan Isles Lighthouse Keepers

Aliases: None
DOB: Unknown
Nationality: Scottish
Active Years: 1900
Victims: 3 (Disappeared)
Location: Flannan Isles, Scotland
MO: Disappearance under unknown circumstances; potentially foul play, natural causes, or abduction
Conviction: Unsolved
Brief biography:

On December 15, 1900, the light from the Flannan Isles Lighthouse was noticed to be out by a passing ship. Further investigation revealed the disappearance of the three lighthouse keepers, Thomas Marshall, James Ducat, and Donald MacArthur. Despite a thorough search, no trace of the men was found. Theories range from a rogue wave sweeping them away to more sinister possibilities. To this day, the mystery remains unsolved.

Florencio Roque Fernández

Aliases: The Vampire of Argentina
DOB: 1935
Nationality: Argentine
Active Years: 1950s
Victims: 15
Location: Monteros, Argentina
MO: Bit victims' throats, drank their blood
Conviction: Declared insane, died in psychiatric institution, 1965
Brief biography:

Florencio Fernández, known as the "Vampire of Argentina," murdered 15 women in Monteros during the 1950s. He would break into homes at night, biting his victims' throats and drinking their blood, believing he was a vampire. Fernández was arrested in 1960 and declared insane due to his delusions. He was confined to a psychiatric institution, where he died a few years later.

Frank Athen Walls

Aliases: None
DOB: October 12, 1967
Nationality: American
Active Years: 1985–1987
Victims: 3 confirmed
Location: Okaloosa County, Florida, USA
MO: Kidnapped, stabbed, and shot victims
Conviction: Sentenced to death, currently in Union Correctional Facility
Brief biography:

Frank Athen Walls, a serial killer active in Florida, is responsible for at least three murders, including those of two burglary victims in 1987. Known for his violent tendencies, Walls first killed in 1985, slitting the throat of a sunbather. He was convicted of multiple murders and is currently serving a death sentence at Union Correctional Facility in Raiford, Florida.

Francis Donald Nemechek

Aliases: None
DOB: 1951
Nationality: American
Active Years: 1974–1976
Victims: 7
Location: Kansas, USA
MO: Abduction, shooting
Conviction: Life imprisonment
Brief biography:

Francis Donald Nemechek is an American serial killer responsible for the deaths of seven people in Kansas during the mid-1970s. His crimes involved abducting and shooting his victims, most of whom were young women. Nemechek was apprehended in 1976 and sentenced to life imprisonment, where he remains to this day.

Fred & Rose West

Aliases: None
DOB: Fred: September 29, 1941; Rose: November 29, 1953
Nationality: British
Active Years: 1967–1987
Victims: 12+ confirmed
Location: Gloucester, England
MO: Kidnapping, sexual abuse, torture, and murder
Conviction: Fred: Suicide in 1995 before trial; Rose: Life imprisonment (1995)
Brief biography:

Fred and Rose West were a notorious British couple responsible for the torture, sexual assault, and murder of at least 12 young women, including two of their own daughters. Over two decades, they lured victims to their home at 25 Cromwell Street, where they were raped, killed, and buried in the basement or garden. Fred hanged himself in prison in 1995 while awaiting trial, and Rose was convicted and sentenced to life imprisonment without the possibility of parole.

Fred Waterfield and David Gore

Aliases: The Killing Cousins
DOB: Waterfield: September 29, 1952; Gore: August 21, 1953
Nationality: American
Active Years: 1981–1983
Victims: 6 confirmed
Location: Florida
MO: Kidnapping, rape, murder of women
Conviction: Gore: Executed (2012); Waterfield: Life imprisonment
Brief biography:

Fred Waterfield and his cousin David Gore were responsible for the abduction, rape, and murder of six women in Florida during the early 1980s. Gore, an auxiliary sheriff's deputy, used his badge to lure victims into their vehicle. The duo was caught after Gore killed one victim in broad daylight, witnessed by a passing cyclist. Gore was executed in 2012, while Waterfield is serving a life sentence.

Frederick Walter Stephen West

Aliases: Fred West
DOB: September 29, 1941
Nationality: British
Active Years: 1967–1987
Victims: 12 confirmed
Location: Gloucester, England
MO: Torture, rape, murder, dismemberment
Conviction: 12 counts of murder, committed suicide in 1995
Brief biography:

Fred West, one of Britain's most infamous serial killers, was responsible for the murders of at least 12 young women, including his own daughter. Along with his wife, Rose West, he ran a "house of horrors" at 25 Cromwell Street in Gloucester, where they tortured, raped, and murdered their victims. Many bodies were buried in the cellar and garden. West was arrested in 1994 but hanged himself in prison before his trial. Rose West was convicted of 10 murders and remains imprisoned.

Chapter Seven: G-List

Gary Leon Ridgway

Aliases: The Green River Killer
DOB: February 18, 1949
Nationality: American
Active Years: 1980s–2001
Victims: 49 confirmed, possibly more
Location: Seattle, Washington, USA
MO: Strangled women, often prostitutes, and dumped bodies in river
Conviction: Life imprisonment without parole (2003)

Brief biography:

Gary Ridgway, known as the "Green River Killer," was convicted of murdering 49 women, though he confessed to as many as 71, making him one of the most prolific serial killers in U.S. history. Ridgway primarily targeted sex workers and runaways, strangling his victims and disposing of their bodies in the Green River or nearby wooded areas. He was arrested in 2001 after DNA evidence linked him to several murders. In a plea deal to avoid the death penalty, Ridgway cooperated with authorities, providing information on many of his victims. He is currently serving life in prison without parole.

Gary Addison Taylor

Aliases: None
DOB: 1936
Nationality: American
Active Years: 1950s–1970s
Victims: 4
Location: Ohio, Washington, Texas, USA
MO: Assaulted and murdered women with hammers and firearms
Conviction: Sentenced to life imprisonment
Brief biography:

Gary Addison Taylor, an American serial killer, attacked women beginning with assaults at bus stops and later escalated to murders across multiple states. Initially using a hammer, he later used firearms, killing at least four women between 1972 and 1975. Despite multiple stints in psychiatric institutions, Taylor was eventually arrested and confessed to the murders, receiving life imprisonment. He openly acknowledged his violent compulsion to harm women.

Gatton Murders

Aliases: None
DOB: Unknown
Nationality: Unknown
Active Years: 1898
Victims: 3 (Michael, Ellen, and Norah Murphy)
Location: Gatton, Queensland, Australia
MO: Shooting, bludgeoning, sexual assault (Ellen and Norah)
Conviction: Unsolved; Theo Farmer considered a suspect but committed suicide in 1900
Brief biography:

The Gatton Murders remain one of Australia's most perplexing unsolved cases. In 1898, siblings Michael, Ellen, and Norah Murphy were found murdered near their family's farm in Gatton, Queensland. Ellen and Norah were raped, and their skulls, along with Michael's, were crushed. Despite a thorough investigation and suspicion surrounding Theo Farmer, the case went cold after Farmer's suicide in 1900. The mystery endures, with many believing a cover-up may have hindered the investigation.

Genene Anne Jones

Aliases: None
DOB: July 13, 1950
Nationality: American
Active Years: 1978–1982
Victims: 11-46 suspected
Location: Texas, USA
MO: Poisoned infants with drugs

Conviction: Sentenced to 99 years + 60 years
Brief biography:

Genene Anne Jones was a pediatric nurse suspected of killing between 11 and 46 infant patients in Texas by injecting lethal doses of drugs like digoxin and succinylcholine, causing cardiac arrest so she could attempt to "save" them and gain praise. She was convicted of two murders and sentenced to consecutive terms of 99 and 60 years in prison.

George Adorno

Aliases: None
DOB: Unknown
Nationality: American
Active Years: 1970s-1980s
Victims: 3 confirmed
Location: Texas, USA
MO: Stabbing
Conviction: Sentenced to life
Brief biography:

George Adorno was a Texas-based serial killer who murdered three women in the late 1970s and early 1980s. He used a knife to stab his victims to death, often targeting women who lived alone. Adorno was apprehended after a lengthy investigation and sentenced to life in prison without parole. His case received national attention due to the brutality of his crimes and the fear he instilled in the local community.

George Nelson

Aliases: Babyface
DOB: 1908
Nationality: American
Active Years: 1930s
Victims: 10+
Location: Chicago, Illinois
MO: Bank robbery, shootouts
Conviction: Killed in 1934
Brief biography:

George "Babyface" Nelson was an American gangster and bank robber known for his youthful appearance and ruthless killing sprees, including numerous bank robberies and violent shootouts with law enforcement. Despite his nickname, Nelson was notorious for his viciousness. He was killed in a shootout with FBI agents in 1934.

Gerald and Charlene Gallego

Aliases: None
DOB: Gerald: July 17, 1946; Charlene: October 10, 1956
Nationality: American
Active Years: 1978–1980
Victims: 10 confirmed victims
Location: Sacramento, California
MO: Kidnapping, rape, and murder
Conviction: Gerald sentenced to death; Charlene served 16 years, released in 1997
Brief biography:

Gerald and Charlene Gallego lured teenage girls into their van, where Gerald raped and murdered them while Charlene participated and watched. The couple was responsible for at least ten murders, with Charlene receiving a lighter sentence in exchange for testifying against Gerald. He was sentenced to death and died in prison. Charlene was released in 1997 after serving 16 years.

Gertraud Arzberger

Aliases: None
DOB: Unknown
Nationality: Austrian
Active Years: 1980s
Victims: 3
Location: Vienna, Austria
MO: Poisoning with arsenic
Conviction: Life in prison
Brief biography:

Gertraud Arzberger, an Austrian serial killer, poisoned three men with arsenic in the 1980s, motivated by financial gain. She lured wealthy older men into relationships before poisoning them. Arzberger was caught after police connected the deaths to unusual traces of arsenic found in the victims. She was sentenced to life imprisonment, which shocked the Austrian public.

Gordon Stewart Northcott

Aliases: None
DOB: November 9, 1906
Nationality: Canadian
Active Years: 1926–1928
Victims: 3–4 known victims
Location: Wineville, California, USA
MO: Kidnapping, sexual abuse, bludgeoning to death
Conviction: Executed by hanging in 1930
Brief biography:

Gordon Stewart Northcott was the perpetrator of the infamous "Wineville Chicken Coop Murders" in California between 1926 and 1928. Northcott lured young boys to his chicken farm, where he sexually abused and murdered them. His nephew, Sanford Clark, was forced to assist in the killings, which came to light after Clark's sister reported her concerns to authorities. Northcott was arrested, sentenced to death, and hanged in 1930.

Gilbert Paul Jordan

Aliases: The Boozing Barber
DOB: December 12, 1931
Nationality: Canadian
Active Years: 1965–1988
Victims: Linked to 8–10 deaths
Location: Vancouver, British Columbia, Canada
MO: Killed women by forcing them to drink fatal amounts of alcohol
Conviction: Convicted of manslaughter; served 6 years
Brief biography:

Gilbert Paul Jordan, known as "The Boozing Barber," was a Canadian serial killer infamous for using alcohol as his murder weapon. Targeting vulnerable women in Vancouver's Downtown Eastside, Jordan would drink with his victims and then force excessive amounts of alcohol down their throats until they died. Linked to 8-

10 deaths, Jordan was finally convicted of manslaughter for one of the deaths and served only six years in prison. He died in 2006.

Gilles de Rais

Aliases: None
DOB: 1404
Nationality: French
Active Years: 1430s–1440
Victims: 100+
Location: France
MO: Torture, murder of children
Conviction: Executed by hanging, 1440
Brief biography:

Gilles de Rais was a French knight who fought alongside Joan of Arc during the Hundred Years' War but was later revealed to be a child murderer. Over the course of a decade, de Rais tortured, raped, and murdered at least 100 children, whom his servants abducted. He was eventually caught and confessed to his crimes under threat of torture. De Rais was hanged for his crimes in 1440. Despite his heinous acts, some considered his final moments as signs of repentance.

Giulia Tofana

Aliases: None
DOB: c. 1653
Nationality: Italian
Active Years: 1670–1719
Victims: Estimated 600
Location: Naples, Italy
MO: Poisoned victims with "Aqua Tofana"
Conviction: Executed by garrote, 1723
Brief biography:

Giulia Tofana was an infamous Italian poisoner responsible for the deaths of an estimated 600 people between 1670 and 1719. She provided a poison, known as "Aqua Tofana," to women seeking to rid themselves of unwanted husbands. Tofana's poison was a mixture of arsenic, lead, and belladonna. Her deadly activities came to an end when she was caught and executed by garrote in 1723.

Graham Young

Aliases: The Teacup Poisoner
DOB: September 7, 1947
Nationality: British
Active Years: 1961–1971
Victims: 3 confirmed, multiple attempted
Location: London and Hertfordshire
MO: Poisoning victims with thallium and antimony
Conviction: Life imprisonment, died in 1990
Brief biography:

Graham Young, known as "The Teacup Poisoner," was an English serial killer fascinated by poisons from a young age. His first known victim was his stepmother in 1962, but he was committed to a psychiatric hospital instead of being imprisoned. Released in 1971, he quickly resumed his activities, poisoning co-workers and killing at least two more people before being caught. His detailed diaries and obsession with poison helped secure his conviction. Young died in prison in 1990 under mysterious circumstances, with some speculating he poisoned himself.

Gusztáv Nemeskeri

Aliases: Katoka Street Killer
DOB: 1955
Nationality: Hungarian
Active Years: 1985–1990
Victims: 6
Location: Budapest, Hungary
MO: Bludgeoning, strangulation
Conviction: Sentenced to life imprisonment
Brief biography:

Gusztáv Nemeskeri, known as the "Katoka Street Killer," was a Hungarian serial killer responsible for a series of brutal murders in Budapest during the 1980s. His modus operandi involved bludgeoning and strangling his victims, most of whom were young women. He was eventually captured, tried, and sentenced to life imprisonment.

Gwendolyn Graham & Catherine May Wood

Aliases: None
DOB: Unknown
Nationality: American
Active Years: 1987
Victims: 5
Location: Alpine Manor Nursing Home, Michigan
MO: Suffocated elderly women, sexual gratification
Conviction: Gwendolyn: Life sentence; Catherine: Reduced sentence
Brief biography:

Gwendolyn Graham and Catherine May Wood, known as the killers of Alpine Manor, were nurse's aides who killed five elderly women in Michigan in 1987. They suffocated their victims and engaged in sexual acts after the murders. The duo was involved in a twisted game, keeping personal items of their victims and choosing victims whose initials spelled "murder." Their relationship deteriorated, leading Wood to confess to her ex-husband, which eventually led to their arrest. Gwendolyn was sentenced to life imprisonment, while Catherine received a reduced sentence for cooperation.

Chapter Eight: H-List

Hall-Mills Murders

Aliases: None
DOB: Unknown
Nationality: Unknown
Active Years: 1922
Victims: 2 (Edward Hall, Eleanor Mills)
Location: New Brunswick, New Jersey, USA
MO: Shooting, throat slashing, mutilation of Eleanor Mills
Conviction: Unsolved; suspects included Hall's wife and brothers, but no charges were filed

Brief biography:

The Hall-Mills murders took place in 1922 when Reverend Edward Hall and choir singer Eleanor Mills were found dead at Lover's Lane in New Jersey. Hall had been shot, while Mills' throat was slashed so deeply she was nearly decapitated. Their bodies were posed to suggest intimacy. Although Hall's wife and her brothers were suspected, no one was ever convicted, and the case remains one of New Jersey's most infamous unsolved crimes.

Hans van Zon

Aliases: None
DOB: April 20, 1942
Nationality: Dutch
Active Years: 1967
Victims: 3 confirmed, several suspected
Location: Netherlands
MO: Bludgeoning, robbery, mutilation
Conviction: Life sentence, later amended to 28.5 years, released 1998

Brief biography:

Hans van Zon, a Dutch serial killer, bludgeoned and mutilated his victims during robberies in the 1960s, targeting wealthy individuals for their valuables. He was convicted of three murders but was suspected of several more. Known for his charm and intelligence, van Zon was released in 1998 after serving 28.5 years in prison. He died later that year from alcohol-related health issues.

Harper Brothers

Aliases: Big Harper, Wiley Harper
DOB: Unknown (1700s)
Nationality: American
Active Years: 1790s
Victims: Estimated 30–50
Location: Tennessee, Kentucky, Illinois
MO: Murder, rape, mutilation of bodies
Conviction: Big Harper killed in 1799; Wiley Harper hanged
Brief biography:

Joshua (Big Harper) and William (Wiley) Harper were infamous murderers and rapists who terrorized Tennessee, Kentucky, and Illinois in the late 1700s. Confessing to over thirty murders, they were suspected of killing many more. Known for their cruelty, even river pirates distanced themselves from their depravity. Big Harper was killed by a posse in 1799, while Wiley Harper was later captured and hanged.

Harvey Louis Carignan

Aliases: The Want-Ad Killer
DOB: May 18, 1927
Nationality: American
Active Years: 1949–1974
Victims: 5 confirmed
Location: North Dakota, Washington, Minnesota, USA
MO: Lured victims via job ads, bludgeoned them with a hammer
Conviction: Serving life sentence in Minnesota Correctional Facility
Brief biography:

Harvey Louis Carignan, known as "The Want-Ad Killer," lured victims by placing want ads for jobs, then brutally bludgeoned them with a hammer. His first known murder occurred in 1949, and his killing spree resumed in the 1970s across several states. He is currently serving a life sentence in Minnesota.

Herbert Arnold

Aliases: None
DOB: 1920
Nationality: German
Active Years: 1940s
Victims: 4
Location: Germany
MO: Stabbing, bludgeoning
Conviction: Life in prison
Brief biography:

Herbert Arnold, a German serial killer, was convicted of murdering four people in post-war Germany, including both acquaintances and strangers whom he attacked in brutal fits of rage. His cold demeanor during the trial shocked the public. Arnold was sentenced to life in prison, where he remained until his death.

Harold Shipman

Aliases: Dr. Death
DOB: January 14, 1946
Nationality: British
Active Years: 1975–1998
Victims: Estimated 215–236
Location: England
MO: Administered lethal doses of morphine to elderly patients
Conviction: Life imprisonment, committed suicide in 2004
Brief biography:

Harold Shipman, known as "Dr. Death," was a British general practitioner and one of history's most prolific serial killers, with estimates of over 200 victims. His patients were mostly elderly women whom he killed by administering fatal doses of morphine. Shipman's crimes were uncovered in 1998 after the suspicious death of a wealthy widow who had left her estate to him. He was convicted of 15 murders but committed suicide in prison in 2004, leading to significant reforms in UK medical practices.

Hélène Jégado

Aliases: None
DOB: 1803
Nationality: French
Active Years: 1833–1851
Victims: 36 confirmed
Location: France
MO: Poisoned victims with arsenic
Conviction: Executed by guillotine, 1852
Brief biography:

Hélène Jégado was a French domestic servant who poisoned at least 36 people over 18 years using arsenic. Her spree began in 1833 and ended with her capture in 1851. Moving from household to household, Jégado left a trail of death behind her, ultimately leading to her execution by guillotine in 1852.

Henry Louis Wallace

Aliases: The Taco Bell Strangler
DOB: November 4, 1965
Nationality: American
Active Years: 1992–1994
Victims: 10
Location: Charlotte, North Carolina, USA
MO: Raped and strangled women, mostly fast-food workers
Conviction: Sentenced to death in 1997, awaiting execution
Brief biography:

Henry Louis Wallace, known as "The Taco Bell Strangler," murdered 10 women in Charlotte, North Carolina, between 1992 and 1994. Many victims were women he knew, including coworkers from fast-food restaurants. Wallace raped and strangled his victims and often attended their funerals afterward. He was arrested in 1994 and sentenced to death in 1997. Wallace remains on death row.

Herbert William Mullin

Aliases: None
DOB: 1947
Nationality: American
Active Years: 1972–1973
Victims: 13
Location: California, USA
MO: Shooting, stabbing, bludgeoning
Conviction: Life imprisonment
Brief biography:

Herbert Mullin was an American serial killer who murdered 13 people during a killing spree in California between 1972 and 1973. Mullin believed he needed to kill to prevent earthquakes, claiming human sacrifice would stop a catastrophic quake. Diagnosed with paranoid schizophrenia, Mullin was sentenced to life imprisonment after his conviction in 1973.

H.H. Holmes

Aliases: H.H. Holmes
DOB: May 16, 1861
Nationality: American
Active Years: 1880s–1894
Victims: Estimated 9 confirmed, possibly 200+
Location: Chicago, Illinois
MO: Lured victims to his "Murder Castle"; torture and murder in specially constructed rooms
Conviction: Executed by hanging in 1896
Brief biography:

H.H. Holmes, considered one of America's first serial killers, is infamous for constructing a "Murder Castle" in Chicago during the 1893 World Fair. The building had secret rooms, hidden passageways, and doors that led nowhere, all designed to disorient and trap victims. Holmes lured his victims, mostly women, to the building where they were tortured and murdered. He sold the skeletons to medical schools and practiced various insurance frauds. Holmes was eventually caught for the murder of his associate, Benjamin Pitezel, and was executed in 1896.

Hinterkaifeck Murders

Aliases: None
DOB: Unknown
Nationality: Unknown
Active Years: 1922
Victims: 6 (Gruber family and maid)
Location: Hinterkaifeck Farm, Bavaria, Germany
MO: Lured to barn, bludgeoned to death
Conviction: Unsolved; no suspects convicted
Brief biography:

The Hinterkaifeck Murders occurred in 1922 at a remote farmstead in Bavaria, Germany, where six people, including the Gruber family and their maid, were killed by an unknown assailant. The killer lured the victims to the barn and bludgeoned them to death, staying at the farm afterward to tend livestock and live in the family's home before disappearing. Despite several arrests, the case remains unsolved and continues to fascinate true crime enthusiasts.

Howard Arthur Allen

Aliases: None
DOB: 1949
Nationality: American
Active Years: 1974-1987
Victims: 3 confirmed
Location: Indiana, USA
MO: Burglary, robbery, and strangulation
Conviction: Sentenced to death
Brief biography:

Howard Arthur Allen was an American serial killer who murdered three elderly women in Indiana between 1974 and 1987. Known for targeting older women, Allen gained entry to their homes under false pretenses, committing burglary, robbery, and strangulation. He was apprehended after the murder of his third victim and sentenced to death in 1988. Allen remains one of the most notorious serial killers in Indiana's history.

Chapter Nine: I-List

Ian Brady & Myra Hindley

Aliases: The Moors Murderers
DOB: Brady: January 2, 1938; Hindley: July 23, 1942
Nationality: British
Active Years: 1963–1965
Victims: 5 confirmed
Location: Manchester, England, UK
MO: Kidnapping, torture, sexual abuse, and murder of children
Conviction: Both sentenced to life imprisonment in 1966

Brief biography:

Ian Brady and Myra Hindley were responsible for the notorious Moors Murders in England. Between 1963 and 1965, the pair lured children and teenagers into their car, where they were sexually assaulted and murdered, with the bodies buried on Saddleworth Moor. The case broke when Hindley's brother-in-law witnessed the murder of Edward Evans, leading to their arrest. Brady was declared criminally insane and confined to Ashworth Hospital, while Hindley remained in prison until her death in 2002. Brady died in 2017.

Ibrahim Hamza Allam

Aliases: None
DOB: Unknown
Nationality: Egyptian
Active Years: 1950s-1960s
Victims: 6 confirmed
Location: Egypt
MO: Poisoning
Conviction: Sentenced to death

Brief biography:

Ibrahim Hamza Allam was an Egyptian serial killer who poisoned six individuals, primarily for financial gain, during the 1950s and 1960s. Posing as a trusted friend or family member, he carried out his crimes undetected until forensic analysis linked him to the murders. Allam was sentenced to death and executed in Egypt, with his case becoming infamous for its deception and greed.

Ion Rîmaru

Aliases: The Vampire of Bucharest
DOB: October 12, 1946
Nationality: Romanian
Active Years: 1970–1971
Victims: 4 murdered, multiple attempted
Location: Bucharest, Romania
MO: Attacked women with hammers and knives, drank blood
Conviction: Executed by firing squad, 1971

Brief biography:

Ion Rîmaru, known as the Vampire of Bucharest, terrorized Romania in 1970–1971 by murdering and mutilating four women. He gained notoriety for biting his victims, drinking their blood, and assaulting them. His spree ended when police found evidence linking him to the crimes. Rîmaru was convicted and executed by firing squad in 1971.

Israel Keyes

Aliases: None
DOB: January 7, 1978
Nationality: American
Active Years: 2001–2012
Victims: 3–11+ confirmed
Location: United States
MO: Kidnapping, murder, pre-planned killings
Conviction: Committed suicide in jail, 2012

Brief biography:

Israel Keyes was an American serial killer known for meticulous planning and a lack of victim profile, committing murders far from home and burying "kill kits" years before using them. He is most notorious for the murder of Bill and Lorraine Currier in Vermont, where he used a kit hidden two years prior. Keyes committed suicide in jail in December 2012 before standing trial, leaving behind many unanswered questions about his crimes.

Ivan Milat

Aliases: The Backpacker Killer
DOB: 1944
Nationality: Australian
Active Years: 1989-1992
Victims: 7
Location: Belanglo State Forest
MO: Stabbing, shooting, bludgeoning
Conviction: Life in prison.

Brief biography:

Ivan Milat, known as the Backpacker Killer, was an Australian serial killer responsible for the deaths of seven backpackers in Belanglo State Forest between 1989 and 1992. Targeting foreign travelers, Milat lured victims to isolated areas where he tortured and killed them. A major manhunt led to his capture, and in 1996, Milat was sentenced to life imprisonment. He died in 2019, leaving a chilling impact on Australia's backpacking tourism industry.

Chapter Ten: J-List

Jack the Ripper

Aliases: The Whitechapel Murderer, Leather Apron
DOB: Unknown
Nationality: Unknown
Active Years: 1888
Victims: 5 canonical victims (possibly more)
Location: London, England (Whitechapel)
MO: Mutilation and disembowelment of female prostitutes
Conviction: Never caught or identified

Brief biography:

Jack the Ripper remains one of history's most infamous and enigmatic serial killers. Operating in the Whitechapel district of London in 1888, he murdered and mutilated at least five female prostitutes. The Ripper's gruesome methods and taunting letters to the press solidified his place in criminal lore. Despite an extensive investigation, he was never caught, fueling over a century of speculation and numerous suspects ranging from doctors to royalty.

Jack Madumetsa Mogale

Aliases: West-End Serial Killer
DOB: 1968
Nationality: South African
Active Years: 2008–2009
Victims: 16 known victims
Location: Westonaria & Lenasia, South Africa
MO: Rape, strangulation, assault
Conviction: 16 life sentences, plus an additional 23 years
Brief biography:

Jack Mogale, the "West-End Serial Killer," terrorized South Africa's Westonaria and Lenasia regions from 2008 to 2009, primarily targeting women. His violent spree included rapes and murders through brutal methods such as strangulation. Captured in 2009, Mogale was convicted of 16 murders and other crimes, and sentenced to 16 life terms in prison, ensuring he would never be released.

Jake Bird

Aliases: Tacoma Axe Killer
DOB: December 14, 1901
Nationality: American
Active Years: 1942–1947
Victims: 44
Location: Multiple states across the USA
MO: Killed victims with axes or hatchets
Conviction: Executed by hanging, July 15, 1949
Brief biography:

Jake Bird, known as the Tacoma Axe Killer, was an American serial killer who claimed to have murdered 44 people across 11 states from 1942 to 1947. Primarily targeting women, he killed his victims with axes or hatchets. Arrested in 1947 in Tacoma, Washington, Bird delayed his execution by confessing to more murders but was eventually hanged in 1949.

Jack Harrison Trawick

Aliases: None
DOB: 1946
Nationality: American
Active Years: 1972–1992
Victims: 5 confirmed (suspected 14)
Location: Alabama, Oregon, USA
MO: Strangulation, stabbing
Conviction: Executed by lethal injection, 2009
Brief biography:

Jack Harrison Trawick, convicted of murdering at least five people, and possibly as many as 14, in Alabama and Oregon, was executed in 2009. Known for strangling, stabbing, or beating his victims, Trawick received the death sentence for the murder of Stephanie Gach in Alabama and was executed by lethal injection.

Jane Toppan

Aliases: Jolly Jane
DOB: March 31, 1854
Nationality: American
Active Years: 1885–1901
Victims: 31 confirmed
Location: Massachusetts, USA
MO: Poisoning with morphine and atropine
Conviction: Not guilty by reason of insanity, 1901
Brief biography:

Jane Toppan, also known as "Jolly Jane," was a nurse and serial killer who admitted to killing 31 people by poisoning them with morphine and atropine. Toppan enjoyed experimenting with doses to observe effects. She was arrested in 1901 and deemed not guilty by reason of insanity, spending the rest of her life in Taunton Insane Hospital until her death in 1938.

James Dale Ritchie

Aliases: None
DOB: 1976
Nationality: American
Active Years: 2016
Victims: 5 confirmed
Location: Alaska, USA
MO: Shooting
Conviction: Killed by police

Brief biography:

James Dale Ritchie, known as the 2016 Anchorage Serial Killer, was responsible for the random shooting deaths of five people in Alaska over several months in 2016. His violent spree ended when he was killed in a shootout with police in November 2016, putting an end to his brief but deadly series of attacks.

Jamison Family

Aliases: None
DOB: Various
Nationality: American
Active Years: 2009-2013
Victims: 3
Location: Red Oak, Oklahoma, USA
MO: Disappearance and suspected murder
Conviction: Unsolved; no arrests made
Brief biography:

The Jamison family—Bobby, Sherilyn, and their six-year-old daughter Madyson—disappeared in October 2009 while looking to buy land in Oklahoma. Their abandoned truck was found with belongings and their family dog left behind. Their remains were found in 2013, but the cause of death remained unclear, and the case is unsolved.

Jean-Charles Avinain

Aliases: The Parisian Assassin
DOB: 1812
Nationality: French
Active Years: 1860s
Victims: 5+
Location: Paris, France
MO: Poisoning, stabbing
Conviction: Executed in 1867
Brief biography:

Jean-Charles Avinain, "The Parisian Assassin," murdered at least five people in Paris during the 1860s, targeting wealthy individuals through charm before poisoning and stabbing them. His ruthlessness and cold methods made him notorious in 19th-century France. He was caught, tried, and executed by guillotine in 1867.

Jeffrey Dahmer

Aliases: The Milwaukee Cannibal
DOB: May 21, 1960
Nationality: American
Active Years: 1978–1991
Victims: 17 confirmed
Location: Milwaukee, Wisconsin, USA
MO: Murder, sexual assault, necrophilia, cannibalism
Conviction: Life imprisonment (1992), murdered in prison (1994)
Brief biography:

Jeffrey Dahmer, the "Milwaukee Cannibal," was responsible for the murders of 17 young men from 1978 to 1991, involving sexual assault, necrophilia, and cannibalism. Arrested in 1991 after a victim escaped and led police to his apartment, Dahmer was sentenced to life imprisonment in 1992. He was murdered by a fellow inmate in 1994.

Jeff Adams

Aliases: None
DOB: Unknown
Nationality: American
Active Years: 2000s
Victims: 3 confirmed
Location: Alabama, USA
MO: Stabbing
Conviction: Sentenced to life
Brief biography:

Jeff Adams is an American serial killer convicted of stabbing three people to death in Alabama in the early 2000s. Captured after a failed attempt to murder another person, which led to his arrest, Adams was sentenced to life without parole. His case remains one of Alabama's most notorious serial killings.

Jeannie Mills

Aliases: People's Temple Defector
DOB: 1939
Nationality: American
Active Years: 1980

Victims: 3 (Jeannie Mills, husband, daughter)
Location: Berkeley, California, USA
MO: Execution-style shooting
Conviction: Unsolved; Jeannie Mills' son suspected but never charged
Brief biography:

Jeannie Mills, a former member of Jim Jones's People's Temple, was murdered along with her husband and daughter in 1980, two years after the Jonestown massacre. They were all shot execution-style in their Berkeley home. Conspiracy theories suggest CIA involvement due to her knowledge of Jim Jones's connections, but others believe her son Eddie was the perpetrator. The case remains unsolved.

Jerry Louis Nemnich

Aliases: None
DOB: 1945
Nationality: American
Active Years: 1975–1990s
Victims: 9+
Location: Colorado, USA
MO: Stabbing, sexual assault
Conviction: Sentenced to life imprisonment
Brief biography:

Jerry Louis Nemnich was convicted of multiple murders, most notably the 1975 killing of Linda Benson and her young daughter in Colorado. Decades later, DNA evidence linked him to the crime. Nemnich is suspected of additional murders and is serving life in prison for his brutal acts.

Jerry K. Thompson

Aliases: None
DOB: March 17, 1961
Nationality: American
Active Years: 1991
Victims: 3 confirmed
Location: Indianapolis, Indiana
MO: Shot during robberies

Conviction: Stabbed to death in prison, 2002
Brief biography:

Jerry K. Thompson was a career criminal who shot and killed three people during robberies in Indianapolis, Indiana, in 1991. His victims included Melvin Hillis, Robert Beeler, and Wesley Crandall. Thompson was sentenced to death but was killed by fellow inmates at Indiana State Prison in 2002.

Jeong Nam-gyu

Aliases: None
DOB: 1969
Nationality: South Korean
Active Years: 2004–2006
Victims: 14
Location: South Korea
MO: Stabbing, home invasion
Conviction: Executed in 2009
Brief biography:

Jeong Nam-gyu was a South Korean serial killer who terrorized the country between 2004 and 2006, killing 14 people in brutal home invasions. He targeted families and used violent stabbing methods. Captured in 2006, Nam-gyu was executed in 2009, leaving behind a notorious criminal legacy in South Korea.

Joe Vance Tilley

Aliases: None
DOB: 1974
Nationality: American
Active Years: 1990
Victims: 3 confirmed
Location: Oklahoma, USA
MO: Stabbed victims
Conviction: Life without parole + death penalty, 1993
Brief biography:

Joe Vance Tilley was convicted of murdering Herman Deagon and two 15-year-old girls in Oklahoma in 1990. He received life without parole for one count of murder and a death sentence for the second. His brutal crimes shocked the local community, and he remains incarcerated.

John Bodkin Adams

Aliases: None
DOB: 1899
Nationality: British
Active Years: 1946-1956
Victims: 163 suspected
Location: England
MO: Poisoning elderly patients
Conviction: Acquitted in 1957
Brief biography:

John Bodkin Adams was a British doctor suspected of being one of the most prolific serial killers in history, linked to the deaths of 163 elderly patients via lethal drug doses. Despite suspicion and a trial, Adams was acquitted in 1957, but his case remains infamous due to the number of suspicious deaths associated with him.

John Brennan Crutchley

Aliases: The Vampire Killer
DOB: October 1, 1946
Nationality: American
Active Years: 1970s–1985
Victims: Suspected 15–20
Location: USA (Florida, Pennsylvania, etc.)
MO: Kidnapped, raped, and drained blood from victims
Conviction: Sentenced to life in prison, died in 2002
Brief biography:

John Brennan Crutchley, also known as the Vampire Killer, was suspected of killing up to 20 women. His method included tying up victims, draining their blood, and drinking it. He was arrested in Florida in 1985 after a victim escaped and alerted authorities. Crutchley was sentenced to life in 1986 and died in prison in 2002.

John Floyd Thomas Jr.

Aliases: Westside Rapist
DOB: July 26, 1936
Nationality: American
Active Years: 1972–1986
Victims: 17 known
Location: Los Angeles, California
MO: Rape and strangulation of elderly women
Conviction: Life imprisonment without parole
Brief biography:

John Floyd Thomas Jr., known as the "Westside Rapist," terrorized Los Angeles by raping and murdering elderly women over more than a decade. His killing spree was long unsolved, only later connected through DNA evidence. Arrested in 2009, he was sentenced to life in 2011, ending his reign of terror.

John George Haigh

Aliases: Acid Bath Murderer
DOB: 1909
Nationality: British
Active Years: 1944-1949
Victims: 6 confirmed
Location: England
MO: Dissolved bodies in acid
Conviction: Executed in 1949
Brief biography:

John George Haigh, known as the Acid Bath Murderer, gained infamy for dissolving his victims' bodies in sulfuric acid after killing them. Haigh believed this method would prevent detection. His plan failed when police found traces of his victims, leading to his conviction and execution in 1949.

John Eric Armstrong

Aliases: None
DOB: 1973
Nationality: American
Active Years: 1992-1999
Victims: 5+

Location: Michigan, USA
MO: Strangulation, sexual assault
Conviction: Life in prison
Brief biography:

John Eric Armstrong, a former U.S. Navy sailor, is a convicted serial killer responsible for the deaths of at least five women in Michigan during the 1990s. Armstrong preyed on sex workers, luring them to secluded areas where he would strangle them. He was arrested in 2000 after a failed murder attempt led to his confession and conviction. Armstrong claimed to have killed more victims across multiple countries, though these claims remain unverified.

John Frederick Thanos

Aliases: None
DOB: March 28, 1949
Nationality: American
Active Years: 1990
Victims: 3 confirmed
Location: Maryland, USA
MO: Shot three robbery victims
Conviction: Executed by lethal injection, 1994

Brief biography:

John Frederick Thanos was an American serial killer who murdered three teenagers during a 1990 robbery spree in Maryland. His victims included Melody Pistorio, Billy Winebrenner, and Gregory Allen Taylor. Thanos was sentenced to death, becoming the first person executed in Maryland since 1976. He died by lethal injection on May 17, 1994.

John Joubert

Aliases: Nebraska Boy Snatcher
DOB: 1963
Nationality: American
Active Years: 1982–1983
Victims: 3
Location: Nebraska, USA

MO: Stabbing, abduction
Conviction: Executed in 1996
Brief biography:

John Joubert, also known as the "Nebraska Boy Snatcher," was an American serial killer who abducted and murdered three young boys in Nebraska between 1982 and 1983. He kidnapped his victims, stabbed them to death, and left their bodies in remote areas. Joubert was arrested, tried, and executed in 1996, and his case remains one of Nebraska's most notorious child-murder cases.

John Reginald Halliday Christie

Aliases: Reg Christie
DOB: April 8, 1899
Nationality: British
Active Years: 1940s–1953
Victims: 8 confirmed
Location: Notting Hill, London
MO: Strangulation and gassing of victims, necrophilia
Conviction: Sentenced to death, hanged in 1953
Brief biography:

John Christie was an English serial killer who murdered at least eight people, including his wife, in his home at 10 Rillington Place. Christie would strangle and later sexually assault his victims' corpses, and his trial exposed flaws in the British legal system, especially after Timothy Evans was wrongly hanged for one of Christie's crimes. This case was a significant factor in the abolition of the death penalty in Britain.

John Duffy and David Mulcahy

Aliases: Railway Killers
DOB: Duffy: November 29, 1958; Mulcahy: January 1959
Nationality: British
Active Years: 1982–1985
Victims: 3 confirmed, 20+ assaults
Location: London, England
MO: Assault, rape, and murder near railways

Conviction: Duffy: Life imprisonment; Mulcahy: Life imprisonment
Brief biography:

Known as the Railway Killers, John Duffy and David Mulcahy were childhood friends who committed a series of rapes and murders near London railway stations in the early 1980s. Responsible for at least three murders and over 20 assaults, Duffy was convicted in 1988. In 1997, he implicated Mulcahy, who was subsequently sentenced to life imprisonment.

John Wayne Gacy

Aliases: The Killer Clown
DOB: March 17, 1942
Nationality: American
Active Years: 1972–1978
Victims: 33+ confirmed
Location: Chicago, Illinois, USA
MO: Lured young men and boys, sexually assaulted, tortured, and strangled them
Conviction: Death sentence (1980), executed in 1994
Brief biography:

John Wayne Gacy, known as "The Killer Clown," murdered at least 33 young men and boys in Chicago. He lured victims to his home, assaulted, and strangled them, burying most of their bodies in his crawl space. Gacy's arrest in 1978 led to his death sentence in 1980, and he was executed by lethal injection in 1994. His crimes are among the most infamous in U.S. history.

Jodi Huisentruit

Aliases: None
DOB: June 5, 1968
Nationality: American
Active Years: 1995
Victims: 1 (disappeared)
Location: Mason City, Iowa, USA
MO: Likely abduction, evidence of struggle
Conviction: Legally declared dead in 2001, case unsolved
Brief biography:

Jodi Huisentruit, a television news anchor, disappeared in 1995 while on her way to work. Evidence at the scene suggested a violent abduction, and despite numerous theories and a warrant for John Vansice's arrest in 2017, the case remains unsolved. Huisentruit was legally declared dead in 2001, though her body has never been found.

Joachim Kroll

Aliases: Ruhr Hunter
DOB: April 17, 1933
Nationality: German
Active Years: 1955–1976
Victims: 14+
Location: West Germany
MO: Murder, necrophilia, cannibalism
Conviction: 9 life sentences, died of a heart attack in 1991
Brief biography:

Joachim Kroll was a German serial killer and cannibal who murdered at least 14 people between 1955 and 1976. Kroll was arrested after a neighbor found clogged pipes filled with human remains. Sentenced to nine life terms, Kroll admitted to consuming parts of his victims, claiming it was a cost-saving measure. He died in prison in 1991.

JonBenét Ramsey

Aliases: None
DOB: August 6, 1990
Nationality: American
Active Years: 1996
Victims: 1
Location: Boulder, Colorado, USA
MO: Strangulation, blunt force trauma
Conviction: Unsolved, no conviction
Brief biography:

JonBenét Ramsey, a 6-year-old beauty pageant contestant, was found murdered in her Boulder, Colorado home in 1996. Despite numerous theories, including suspicion of family involvement, the case remains unsolved, and JonBenét's death is one of the most infamous unsolved murders in U.S. history.

Johann "Jack" Unterweger

Aliases: Vienna Strangler
DOB: August 16, 1950
Nationality: Austrian
Active Years: 1974, 1990-1992
Victims: 11 confirmed
Location: Austria, USA
MO: Strangulation with victims' bras
Conviction: Life imprisonment, committed suicide in 1994
Brief biography:

Jack Unterweger, the Vienna Strangler, was a convicted murderer who, after being released, resumed killing women in Austria and the U.S., strangling them with their own bras. He was arrested in 1992, convicted of 11 murders, and took his own life in prison in 1994, leaving behind a legacy of manipulation and betrayal of public trust.

Joseph L. Taborsky and Arthur Culombe

Aliases: None
DOB: Taborsky: March 23, 1924; Culombe: 1923
Nationality: American
Active Years: 1951–1957
Victims: 6
Location: Connecticut, USA
MO: Shot victims during robberies
Conviction: Taborsky: Executed in 1960 by electric chair; Culombe: Sentenced to life imprisonment
Brief biography:

Joseph Taborsky and Arthur Culombe were responsible for a string of deadly robberies in Connecticut, killing six people by shooting them. Taborsky was executed in 1960, becoming the last person executed by electric chair in Connecticut, while Culombe received a life sentence.

Joseph Philippe

Aliases: Terror of Paris
DOB: 1835
Nationality: French
Active Years: 1861–1866
Victims: 7 prostitutes, 1 child
Location: Paris, France
MO: Murder and strangulation
Conviction: Executed by guillotine in 1866
Brief biography:

Joseph Philippe, called the "Terror of Paris," killed seven female prostitutes and a 10-year-old child between 1861 and 1866. His crimes spread fear across Paris until his arrest and conviction. Philippe was executed by guillotine in July 1866, leaving behind a notorious legacy of terror.

Joseph Ture

Aliases: None
DOB: February 7, 1951
Nationality: American
Active Years: 1978–1981
Victims: 6 confirmed
Location: Minnesota, USA
MO: Bludgeoning, abduction
Conviction: Life imprisonment (multiple counts), 1998–2000
Brief biography:

Joseph Ture was a violent criminal who murdered six individuals in Minnesota between 1978 and 1981. His victims included a mother, her three children, and two additional women. Ture used methods like bludgeoning and abduction. Convicted in 1998 and 2000, he is serving multiple life sentences.

Joseph Vacher

Aliases: None
DOB: November 16, 1869
Nationality: French
Active Years: 1894–1897
Victims: 11–27
Location: France
MO: Stabbed, mutilated, raped victims
Conviction: Executed by guillotine, 1898
Brief biography:

Joseph Vacher, a French serial killer, murdered between 11 and 27 people, primarily adolescent farm workers, from 1894 to 1897. Known for his extreme violence and brutality, Vacher was eventually captured and declared sane. He was guillotined in 1898, ending his reign of terror.

José Dorangel Vargas Gomez

Aliases: None
DOB: May 14, 1956
Nationality: Venezuelan
Active Years: 1998-1999
Victims: 10-14 confirmed
Location: San Cristobal, Venezuela
MO: Cannibalism, hunting victims with spears or rocks
Conviction: Imprisoned, involved in a 2016 prison riot where he killed again
Brief biography:

José Dorangel Vargas Gomez, a Venezuelan cannibal, murdered and ate at least 10 men, targeting victims along riverbanks. He was caught in 1999, convicted, and imprisoned for life. In 2016, during a prison riot, he killed three inmates, continuing his violent streak.

Joshua Julius Anderson

Aliases: None
DOB: 1975
Nationality: American

Active Years: 2000-2001
Victims: 2
Location: Florida, USA
MO: Shooting
Conviction: Life in prison
Brief biography:

Joshua Julius Anderson was convicted of two execution-style murders during a robbery spree in Florida in 2000. Captured based on witness testimony and security footage, he was sentenced to life in prison in 2002.

Joshua Wade

Aliases: None
DOB: 1980
Nationality: American
Active Years: 2000-2007
Victims: 4 confirmed
Location: Alaska, USA
MO: Rape, stabbing
Conviction: Life imprisonment
Brief biography:

Joshua Wade, the Anchorage Serial Killer, murdered four women in Alaska, primarily during burglaries. His violent methods included rape and stabbing. Arrested in 2007, Wade was sentenced to life in prison without parole.

Joseph Dewey Akin

Aliases: None
DOB: 1954
Nationality: American
Active Years: 1980s-1990s
Victims: 4 confirmed
Location: Alabama, USA
MO: Poisoning (insulin)
Conviction: Sentenced to life
Brief biography:

Joseph Dewey Akin, a nurse, used his medical knowledge to kill at least four patients through insulin overdoses. Active in Alabama during the 1980s and 1990s, his crimes were uncovered through hospital investigations, leading to his life sentence.

Joseph Naso

Aliases: Alphabet Killer
DOB: 1934
Nationality: American
Active Years: 1970s–1990s
Victims: 6
Location: California, USA
MO: Strangulation, murder
Conviction: Sentenced to death
Brief biography:

Joseph Naso, known as the "Alphabet Killer," murdered at least six women whose initials matched (like "C.C." or "R.R.") over decades. His crimes were discovered in 2010 when incriminating evidence was found in his home, resulting in a death sentence.

Jose Munoz

Aliases: None
DOB: Unknown
Nationality: American
Active Years: 1992
Victims: 3
Location: California, USA
MO: Stabbing
Conviction: Sentenced to life in prison
Brief biography:

Jose Munoz murdered three people through brutal stabbings in California in 1992. Captured after his final murder, Munoz was sentenced to life imprisonment, where he remains for his crimes.

Juan Rodriguez Chavez

Aliases: Thrill Killer
DOB: April 27, 1968
Nationality: American
Active Years: 1995
Victims: 12 confirmed
Location: Texas, USA
MO: Shot and killed victims during robberies
Conviction: Executed by lethal injection, April 22, 2003
Brief biography:

Juan Rodriguez Chavez was a serial killer who murdered 12 people in Texas during a 1995 killing spree. He conducted robberies that turned violent, killing victims by shooting or even running them over. Chavez was convicted of capital murder and executed in 2003.

Chapter Eleven: K-List

Karla Homolka and Paul Bernardo

Aliases: None
DOB: Homolka: May 4, 1970; Bernardo: August 27, 1964
Nationality: Canadian
Active Years: 1990–1992
Victims: 3 confirmed
Location: Ontario, Canada
MO: Rape, torture, and murder of young women
Conviction: Homolka served 12 years; Bernardo sentenced to life imprisonment

Brief biography:

Karla Homolka and Paul Bernardo were a Canadian couple responsible for the brutal rapes and murders of three young women, including Karla's sister Tammy. Bernardo was also identified as the Scarborough Rapist. Karla secured a plea deal for a 12-year sentence by testifying against Bernardo, who remains in prison for life. Since her release, Karla has remarried and kept a low profile.

Keddie Cabin Murders

Aliases: None
DOB: Unknown
Nationality: American
Active Years: 1981
Victims: 4 (including Tina Sharp)
Location: Cabin 28, Keddie, California, USA
MO: Bludgeoning and stabbing
Conviction: Unsolved; suspects Marty Smartt and Bo Boubede were never charged
Brief biography:

In April 1981, the Sharp family and a friend were violently murdered at a cabin in Keddie, California. Twelve-year-old Tina Sharp went missing and was later found dead. Although Marty Smartt and Bo Boubede were suspected, no charges were filed, and the case remains one of California's most notorious unsolved crimes.

Kenyon Battles Tolerton

Aliases: None
DOB: 1956
Nationality: American
Active Years: 1980–1993
Victims: 3 confirmed
Location: Colorado, USA
MO: Stabbing, rape
Conviction: Life sentence plus 48 years
Brief biography:

Kenyon Tolerton was convicted of murdering three girls in Colorado. After his initial conviction in 1980, he was paroled in 1991, only to kill again in 1993. DNA evidence linked him to the crimes, resulting in a life sentence plus 48 years.

Kevin Taylor

Aliases: None
DOB: June 11, 1974
Nationality: American
Active Years: 2001
Victims: 4
Location: Chicago, Illinois, USA
MO: Strangulation, body disposal in alleys
Conviction: Life in prison
Brief biography:

Kevin Taylor killed at least four women in 2001, targeting vulnerable individuals and leaving their bodies in abandoned areas around Chicago. Convicted on multiple murder counts, Taylor was sentenced to life in prison.

Ken McElroy (Skidmore's Vigilante Justice)

Aliases: None
DOB: 1934

Nationality: American
Active Years: 1981
Victims: 1 (Ken McElroy)
Location: Skidmore, Missouri
MO: Shot by a vigilante mob
Conviction: Unsolved
Brief biography:

Ken McElroy terrorized Skidmore, Missouri, for years before a vigilante group killed him in broad daylight in 1981. Despite numerous witnesses, no one was charged, marking this as one of the most infamous cases of vigilante justice in modern America.

Kenneth Bianchi and Angelo Buono

Aliases: The Hillside Stranglers
DOB: Bianchi: May 22, 1951; Buono: October 5, 1934
Nationality: American
Active Years: 1977–1978
Victims: Estimated 10
Location: Los Angeles, California
MO: Kidnap, rape, torture, and murder of women
Conviction: Bianchi: Life imprisonment; Buono: Life imprisonment
Brief biography:

The Hillside Stranglers, Kenneth Bianchi and Angelo Buono, kidnapped, raped, and murdered multiple women in Los Angeles. Posing as undercover cops, they preyed on vulnerable young women. Bianchi was eventually caught and testified against Buono; both received life sentences.

Kelly Ray Thompson

Aliases: None
DOB: 1968
Nationality: American
Active Years: 1990s
Victims: 8 confirmed
Location: Washington, Colorado
MO: Murder of women

Conviction: 31 years in Washington, 1998
Brief biography:

Kelly Ray Thompson confessed to murdering eight women across Washington and Colorado. Known for brutal violence, he was arrested and sentenced to 31 years in 1998 and remains in prison.

Klaas Annink (Huttenkloas)

Aliases: Huttenkloas
DOB: 1710
Nationality: Dutch
Active Years: 1779
Victims: 1 confirmed, suspected of more
Location: Twente, Netherlands
MO: Robbery, bludgeoning
Conviction: Executed in 1779
Brief biography:

Klaas Annink, or "Huttenkloas," was a feared Dutch criminal. Convicted for murdering a traveling salesman, he was also suspected of other murders. Known for his brutality, Annink was executed by hanging in 1779.

Chapter Twelve: L-List

Larry Hall

Aliases: None
DOB: December 11, 1962
Nationality: American
Active Years: 1980s–1994
Victims: Suspected of 30+
Location: Midwest U.S. (primarily Illinois, Indiana)
MO: Kidnapping and strangulation
Conviction: Life imprisonment for the kidnapping of Jessica Lynn Roach

Brief biography:

Larry Hall is suspected of being one of the most prolific serial killers in U.S. history, with potential responsibility for over thirty murders of women and girls in the Midwest. Despite initial confessions to multiple murders, he later recanted. Hall remains in prison, serving a life sentence for kidnapping, though suspicion still lingers that his twin brother, Gary, may know more than he's revealed.

Larry Lee Ranes and Danny Arthur Ranes

Aliases: None
DOB: Unknown
Nationality: American
Active Years: 1960s–1970s
Victims: 4 confirmed, suspected 10+
Location: Michigan
MO: Kidnapping, murder, dismemberment
Conviction: Larry: Life imprisonment; Danny: Died in 2022

Brief biography:

Brothers Larry Lee Ranes and Danny Arthur Ranes killed separately but both embarked on their own brutal crime sprees in Michigan. Larry was convicted of a single murder but suspected of several more, while Danny was convicted with his partner Brent Koster of multiple murders. Danny passed away in prison in 2022, while Larry remains incarcerated.

Las Poquianchis (The González Sisters)

Aliases: Las Poquianchis
DOB: Unknown
Nationality: Mexican
Active Years: 1950s–1960s
Victims: 91+ suspected victims
Location: Mexico
MO: Starvation, beatings, forced prostitution
Conviction: 40 years imprisonment each
Brief biography:

The González sisters, collectively known as Las Poquianchis, ran brothels in Mexico, luring young women with promises of work before forcing them into prostitution and addiction. They killed their victims through starvation and beatings, with 91 bodies found on their property. The sisters received 40-year sentences, and their case remains one of Mexico's most horrific.

Leszek Jacek Pekalski (The Vampire of Bytow)

Aliases: The Vampire of Bytow
DOB: February 12, 1966
Nationality: Polish
Active Years: 1984–1992
Victims: Confessed to 70, convicted of 1
Location: Poland
MO: Rape and murder
Conviction: 25 years in a psychiatric institution, released under review
Brief biography:

Leszek Pekalski confessed to killing 70 people, earning him the title of "The Vampire of Bytow," but was convicted of only one murder due to lack of evidence. His crimes were marked by extreme brutality, and he was sentenced to 25 years in a psychiatric institution. His case remains controversial in Poland.

Leslie Torres

Aliases: None
DOB: 1971
Nationality: American
Active Years: 1988
Victims: 5 confirmed
Location: New York City, USA
MO: Shot victims during robberies
Conviction: Life sentence, 1989
Brief biography:

Leslie Torres went on a violent spree in New York City, killing five people during robberies in 1988. His crimes were fueled by drug addiction, and he was sentenced to life in prison in 1989, with a minimum term of 60 years.

Lawrence Bittaker and Roy Norris

Aliases: None
DOB: Bittaker: September 27, 1940; Norris: February 5, 1948
Nationality: American
Active Years: 1979
Victims: 5 young women
Location: California
MO: Abduction, rape, torture, murder
Conviction: Bittaker: Death (died in 2019); Norris: 45 years to life
Brief biography:

The "Tool Box Killers" Lawrence Bittaker and Roy Norris carried out heinous acts against five young women, torturing and recording their victims' screams. Bittaker received the death penalty, while Norris was given a reduced sentence for testifying against him. Bittaker died in 2019; Norris remains incarcerated.

Lazarus Tshidiso Mazingane (Nasrec Strangler)

Aliases: Nasrec Strangler
DOB: 1964
Nationality: South African
Active Years: 1996–1997
Victims: 8
Location: South Africa
MO: Strangulation, sexual assault
Conviction: Life imprisonment
Brief biography:

Lazarus Tshidiso Mazingane terrorized Johannesburg, strangling and sexually assaulting eight women. Known as the Nasrec Strangler, he was apprehended in 1997 and is serving a life sentence. His trial received significant attention in South Africa.

Leonard John Fraser (Rockhampton Rapist)

Aliases: Rockhampton Rapist
DOB: 1951
Nationality: Australian
Active Years: 1998-1999
Victims: 4+
Location: Queensland, Australia
MO: Rape, strangulation, mutilation
Conviction: Life in prison
Brief biography:

Leonard John Fraser, a convicted rapist, murdered at least four women in Queensland, Australia. Known for targeting both adults and children, his brutal crimes included rape and mutilation. Fraser died in prison in 2007.

Lisa Jane Turner

Aliases: None
DOB: 1956
Nationality: New Zealander
Active Years: 1980–1984
Victims: 5 children
Location: Christchurch, New Zealand

MO: Smothering
Conviction: Life in prison, paroled in 1997
Brief biography:

Lisa Jane Turner killed five young children in Christchurch, including her own daughters and children she babysat. She was discovered after a neighbor's 8-month-old son died in her care. Sentenced to life imprisonment, Turner was paroled in 1997.

Louis van Schoor

Aliases: None
DOB: 1951
Nationality: South African
Active Years: 1980s
Victims: 39 confirmed, 100+ shot
Location: East London, South Africa
MO: Shooting (hired gunman)
Conviction: 20 years in prison, served 12 years, released 2004
Brief biography:

Louis van Schoor, a South African security guard, shot over 100 people during apartheid, with at least 39 fatalities. He was hired to protect white-owned businesses and targeted Black victims. Convicted in 1992, he served 12 years and was released in 2004.

Long Island Serial Killer (Gilgo Beach Killer)

Aliases: Long Island Serial Killer
DOB: Unknown
Nationality: Unknown
Active Years: 1996–2010
Victims: 10-16+
Location: Long Island, New York
MO: Strangulation; victims wrapped in burlap and buried
Conviction: Ongoing investigation, no conviction yet
Brief biography:

The Long Island Serial Killer is believed to be responsible for the murders of between 10 and 16 individuals, mainly targeting sex workers. The victims' bodies were discovered along Ocean Parkway in Long Island. Although Rex Heuermann has been arrested in connection with the murders, a conviction has not yet been reached, leaving this case as one of the U.S.'s most notorious unsolved serial killer cases.

Louise Vermilyea

Aliases: None
DOB: July 1868
Nationality: American
Active Years: 1893-1911
Victims: 6 suspected
Location: Illinois, USA
MO: Poisoning with arsenic
Conviction: Arrested; no convictions due to hung juries, charges dropped
Brief biography:

Louise Vermilyea was suspected of poisoning six family members and acquaintances with arsenic between 1893 and 1911, including husbands and stepchildren. Although arrested and charged multiple times, her cases ended in hung juries, leading to dropped charges. She was released in 1913, and her whereabouts and activities thereafter remain unknown.

Lowell Edwin Amos

Aliases: None
DOB: 1943
Nationality: American
Active Years: 1979-1994
Victims: 3 confirmed
Location: Michigan, USA
MO: Poisoning
Conviction: Life imprisonment
Brief biography:

Lowell Edwin Amos, a Michigan businessman, poisoned three of his wives between 1979 and 1994 to collect life insurance benefits. He carefully staged each death as accidental, avoiding suspicion until inconsistencies surrounding his third wife's death led to his conviction. Amos is serving a life sentence.

Ludwig Tessnow

Aliases: None
DOB: February 15, 1872
Nationality: German
Active Years: 1898-1901
Victims: 4 children confirmed
Location: Wallenhorst, Germany
MO: Butchering children, mutilation
Conviction: Executed by guillotine in 1904
Brief biography:

Ludwig Tessnow, a German carpenter, gruesomely murdered four children between 1898 and 1901. His crimes ended when testing confirmed bloodstains on his clothes matched human blood. Convicted of his crimes, he was executed by guillotine in 1904.

Lyda Catherine Ambrose (The American Borgia)

Aliases: The American Borgia
DOB: 1890
Nationality: American
Active Years: 1917-1921
Victims: 4 confirmed
Location: Idaho, USA
MO: Poisoning
Conviction: Sentenced to life imprisonment
Brief biography:

Known as "The American Borgia," Lyda Catherine Ambrose poisoned four of her husbands, collecting insurance payouts. Her crimes were uncovered after her fourth husband's death raised suspicions. She was convicted and sentenced to life imprisonment, becoming infamous for her cold-blooded tactics.

Lydia Sherman (Queen Poisoner)

Aliases: Queen Poisoner
DOB: 1824
Nationality: American
Active Years: 1864-1871
Victims: 9 confirmed
Location: Connecticut, USA
MO: Poisoning with arsenic
Conviction: Sentenced to life imprisonment in 1872
Brief biography:

Lydia Sherman poisoned nine people, including three husbands and six children, using arsenic over several years. She avoided suspicion until her final arrest, earning her the moniker "Queen Poisoner." In 1872, she was sentenced to life imprisonment for her calculated murders.

Chapter Thirteen: M-List

Manuel Delgado Villegas (The Arropiero)

Aliases: The Arropiero
DOB: January 25, 1943
Nationality: Spanish
Active Years: 1964-1971
Victims: 7 confirmed, up to 48 suspected
Location: Spain, Italy, France
MO: Strangulation, bludgeoning with hands or weapons
Conviction: Declared criminally insane, institutionalized, no formal conviction

Brief biography:

Manuel Delgado Villegas, dubbed "The Arropiero," is considered one of Spain's most prolific serial killers, suspected in up to 48 murders across Europe. Living as a transient, he used his strength to kill victims with a hand strike to the throat or by bludgeoning. Arrested in 1971, he was declared insane and was institutionalized for life, never formally convicted in court due to his mental condition.

Marcelo Costa de Andrade (Vampire of Niterio)

Aliases: Vampire of Niterio
DOB: January 2, 1967
Nationality: Brazilian
Active Years: 1991
Victims: 14
Location: Rio de Janeiro, Brazil
MO: Strangulation, sexual assault, necrophilia, sometimes cannibalism
Conviction: Confined to Henrique Roxo Psychiatric Hospital, deemed insane

Brief biography:

Marcelo Costa de Andrade, known as the "Vampire of Niterio," horrified Brazil with his brutal murders of 14 boys in 1991. His disturbing methods included rape, strangulation, necrophilia, and occasional cannibalism, primarily targeting street children. After a survivor exposed him, Andrade was deemed insane and remains confined in a psychiatric hospital.

Martha Beck and Raymond Fernandez (The Lonely Hearts Killers)

Aliases: The Lonely Hearts Killers
DOB: Martha: May 6, 1920; Raymond: December 17, 1914
Nationality: American
Active Years: 1947–1949
Victims: 3 confirmed, suspected 20+
Location: U.S. (New York to Michigan)
MO: Lured women through lonely hearts ads, then murdered them
Conviction: Both sentenced to death, executed in 1951
Brief biography:

Martha Beck and Raymond Fernandez used lonely hearts ads to lure women before robbing and killing them. Beck posed as Fernandez's sister, gaining their victims' trust. They were eventually caught in Michigan, extradited to New York, and sentenced to death. Their shared affection continued until their execution in 1951.

Maria Catherina Swanenburg (Goeie Mie)

Aliases: Goeie Mie
DOB: September 9, 1839
Nationality: Dutch
Active Years: 1880-1883
Victims: 27 proven, suspected of 90+
Location: Netherlands
MO: Poisoned victims with arsenic
Conviction: Life imprisonment
Brief biography:

Maria Swanenburg, known as "Goeie Mie," was a Dutch serial killer who poisoned at least 27 people with arsenic, often family or people under her care, for life insurance money. Convicted of three murders, she was suspected of killing dozens more. Swanenburg was sentenced to life imprisonment in 1885.

Marie Besnard (Queen of Poisoners)

Aliases: Queen of Poisoners
DOB: 1896
Nationality: French
Active Years: 1920s-1940s
Victims: 12+
Location: Loudun, France
MO: Poisoning with arsenic
Conviction: Acquitted in 1961
Brief biography:

Marie Besnard was charged with poisoning at least 12 individuals, including her husband, using arsenic. Her prolonged trial captivated France, but she was acquitted in 1961 for lack of evidence. Despite her acquittal, many still regard her as responsible for the deaths.

Maria Velten

Aliases: None
DOB: 1916
Nationality: German
Active Years: 1963-1983
Victims: 5
Location: West Germany
MO: Poisoning with arsenic
Conviction: Life imprisonment, later released to a nursing home
Brief biography:

Maria Velten poisoned five family members over two decades with arsenic. Suspicion arose after her last husband's death in 1983, and she was convicted. Velten spent her remaining years in prison, later being moved to a nursing home due to illness before her death in 2008.

Mary Ann Cotton

Aliases: None
DOB: October 1832
Nationality: British

Active Years: 1865-1872
Victims: 21 suspected, convicted of 1
Location: England
MO: Poisoned victims with arsenic
Conviction: Sentenced to death by hanging
Brief biography:

Mary Ann Cotton, suspected of killing 21 people, including husbands and children, poisoned them with arsenic for life insurance benefits. Suspicion arose after a doctor found arsenic in her stepson's remains. Convicted of his murder, she was hanged in 1873, marking her as Britain's first recorded female serial killer.

Marybeth Tinning

Aliases: None
DOB: September 11, 1942
Nationality: American
Active Years: 1971-1985
Victims: 9 confirmed (children)
Location: Schenectady, New York, USA
MO: Smothering
Conviction: 20 years to life, released in 2018
Brief biography:

Marybeth Tinning killed nine of her children over 14 years, smothering many and often attributing their deaths to natural causes. In 1985, she confessed to smothering her infant daughter, Tami Lynne, and was convicted. Tinning was sentenced to 20 years to life and paroled in 2018.

Martha Needle

Aliases: None
DOB: 1863
Nationality: Australian
Active Years: 1885-1894
Victims: 5
Location: Victoria, Australia
MO: Poisoning

Conviction: Executed in 1894
Brief biography:

Martha Needle poisoned five individuals, including family members, between 1885 and 1894 to gain life insurance payouts. Her pattern was uncovered, leading to her conviction and execution by hanging in 1894.

Mary Reeser

Aliases: None
DOB: 1884
Nationality: American
Active Years: 1951
Victims: 1 (Mary Reeser)
Location: St. Petersburg, Florida
MO: Possible spontaneous combustion or fire
Conviction: Unsolved
Brief biography:

Mary Reeser was found almost completely incinerated in her Florida apartment in 1951, with only a portion of her left foot intact. Speculation about her death ranged from falling asleep with a cigarette to spontaneous combustion, but no definitive cause was established, leaving the case an unsolved mystery.

Mary Cecilia Rogers

Aliases: None
DOB: 1820?
Nationality: American
Active Years: 1841
Victims: 1
Location: New York City, USA
MO: Beaten, body found in the Hudson River
Conviction: Unsolved
Brief biography:

Mary Rogers, a popular cigar girl in New York, disappeared in 1841 and was later found in the Hudson River. Her brutal murder stunned the public, and although her fiancé was a suspect, no arrests were made. Edgar Allan Poe based his story "The

Mystery of Marie Rogêt" on her case, which remains one of New York's most famous unsolved murders.

Maury Troy Travis

Aliases: None
DOB: October 25, 1965
Nationality: American
Active Years: 2001–2002
Victims: 12 confirmed, claimed 17
Location: Missouri, USA
MO: Strangulation, torture
Conviction: Committed suicide in prison, 2002
Brief biography:

Maury Troy Travis was an American serial killer in Ferguson, Missouri, who murdered at least 12 women, though he claimed 17 victims. He lured victims to a torture chamber in his basement. Police traced an anonymous map he sent to a newspaper, leading to his arrest. Travis took his life in jail before his trial.

Metod Trobec (Monster of Gorejne Vasi)

Aliases: Monster of Gorejne Vasi
DOB: June 6, 1948
Nationality: Slovenian
Active Years: 1977–1979
Victims: 5 confirmed
Location: Slovenia
MO: Rape, murder, cremation of bodies
Conviction: Death sentence, commuted to 35 years
Brief biography:

Metod Trobec, known as the "Monster of Gorejne Vasi," raped and murdered five women, cremating their remains in his oven. His arrest followed the discovery of human bones in his home. Initially sentenced to death, his sentence was commuted to 35 years. Trobec hanged himself in prison in 2006.

Michael Allen

Aliases: None
DOB: Unknown
Nationality: American
Active Years: 2000s
Victims: 4 confirmed
Location: USA
MO: Strangulation
Conviction: Life imprisonment
Brief biography:

Michael Allen was an American serial killer in the early 2000s, convicted of strangling four women he lured into his car. DNA evidence linked him to multiple scenes, leading to a life sentence without parole.

Michael Devern Terry

Aliases: None
DOB: 1960
Nationality: American
Active Years: 1985–1986
Victims: 6 confirmed
Location: Atlanta, Georgia
MO: Shot and stabbed gay men after sex
Conviction: Life without parole, sentenced 1987
Brief biography:

Michael Devern Terry targeted gay men in Atlanta between 1985 and 1986, killing six after sexual encounters. Convicted in 1987, he was sentenced to life imprisonment without parole.

Michael Tenneson

Aliases: None
DOB: November 21, 1959
Nationality: American
Active Years: 1987
Victims: 5
Location: Colorado and Wisconsin, USA
MO: Robbery, shooting

Conviction: Multiple life terms
Brief biography:

Michael Tenneson, a fugitive, murdered five people across Colorado and Wisconsin in 1987 during a robbery spree. He was convicted and sentenced to life in both states, ending his crime spree.

Mikhail Novosyolov (Necrophile Rebel)

Aliases: Necrophile Rebel
DOB: 1942
Nationality: Russian
Active Years: 1977–1995
Victims: 22
Location: Russia
MO: Strangulation, necrophilia
Conviction: Life imprisonment
Brief biography:

Mikhail Novosyolov, known as the "Necrophile Rebel," strangled and desecrated 22 victims over nearly two decades in Russia. He was convicted and sentenced to life in prison, marking one of Russia's most disturbing criminal cases.

Miyazawa Family Murders

Aliases: None
DOB: Various
Nationality: Japanese
Active Years: 2000
Victims: 4
Location: Setagaya, Tokyo, Japan
MO: Stabbing, strangulation
Conviction: Unsolved
Brief biography:

The Miyazawa family was murdered on December 30, 2000, in Tokyo. The killer stayed at their home, leaving forensic evidence behind. Despite extensive efforts, no suspect has been convicted, and the case remains a chilling mystery in Japan.

Miyoko Sumida (Amagasaki Serial Killer)

Aliases: Amagasaki Serial Killer
DOB: 1947
Nationality: Japanese
Active Years: 1990s-2010s
Victims: 6 confirmed
Location: Japan
MO: Torture, imprisonment
Conviction: Life imprisonment
Brief biography:

Miyoko Sumida led a group that tortured and killed at least six people, manipulating and imprisoning victims. Her crimes were uncovered in 2011, resulting in a life sentence. Sumida committed suicide in jail in 2012.

Mohammad Bijeh (Vampire of Tehran Desert)

Aliases: Vampire of Tehran Desert
DOB: February 7, 1975
Nationality: Iranian
Active Years: 2004
Victims: 16 confirmed, 2 adults
Location: South of Tehran, Iran
MO: Poisoning, sexual assault, murder of children
Conviction: 100 lashes, publicly hanged in 2005
Brief biography:

Mohammad Bijeh, the "Vampire of Tehran Desert," was an Iranian serial killer and rapist responsible for killing 16 boys and 2 adults in 2004. He was publicly lashed and hanged in 2005, marking a rare instance of public execution for serial murder in Iran.

Mohammed Halabi

Aliases: Tel Aviv Strangler
DOB: 1957
Nationality: Palestinian
Active Years: 1989

Victims: 7
Location: Tel Aviv and Jaffa, Israel
MO: Strangulation
Conviction: Sentenced to life imprisonment plus 40 years
Brief biography:

Mohammed Halabi, known as the "Tel Aviv Strangler," was a Palestinian serial killer responsible for the murders of seven individuals in 1989. His victims, comprising both Jewish and Arab residents, were strangled in Tel Aviv and Jaffa, intensifying existing tensions in the region. Following his arrest, Halabi confessed to the murders, which included both men and women. He was sentenced to life imprisonment, with an additional 40 years added due to the severity of his crimes.

Chapter Fourteen: N-List

Nathan Nicholas Trupp

Aliases: N/A
DOB: 1947
Nationality: American
Active Years: 1975–1980
Victims: 5 confirmed
Location: New Mexico, USA; California
MO: Stalking, shooting, and stabbing
Conviction: Committed to a state hospital for life

Brief biography:

Nathan Nicholas Trupp, driven by severe delusions, believed actor Michael Landon was a Nazi and committed five murders, including the killings of two guards at Universal Studios and three individuals in Albuquerque, New Mexico. Found not guilty by reason of insanity, he was committed to a state hospital for life.

Nathaniel White

Aliases: None
DOB: July 28, 1960
Nationality: American
Active Years: 1991–1992
Victims: 6 known victims
Location: Hudson Valley, New York
MO: Abduction, stabbing, and beating victims
Conviction: Sentenced to 150 years to life in prison
Brief biography:

Nathaniel White was convicted of murdering six women in Hudson Valley, New York, between 1991 and 1992, using promises and personal connections to lure his victims. His brutal methods included stabbing and blunt force trauma. White's spree ended after his arrest in 1992, and he remains incarcerated, serving a 150-year sentence.

Norio Nagayama

Aliases: None
DOB: 1949
Nationality: Japanese
Active Years: 1968
Victims: 4
Location: Japan
MO: Shooting
Conviction: Executed in 1997
Brief biography:

Norio Nagayama, a Japanese teenage drifter, committed four murders during a spree of robberies in 1968 using a stolen handgun. His case spurred debate in Japan on juvenile crime and the death penalty. Sentenced to death, he was executed in 1997.

Nicolas Claux (Vampire of Paris)

Aliases: The Vampire of Paris
DOB: March 22, 1972
Nationality: French
Active Years: 1994
Victims: 1 proven, 7 suspected
Location: Paris, France
MO: Grave robbery, murder, cannibalism, blood-drinking
Conviction: 12 years in prison, released March 22, 2002
Brief biography:

Nicolas Claux, a French murderer, grave robber, and cannibal, became known as the "Vampire of Paris" following his 1994 conviction for murdering Thierry Bissonnier. He robbed graves, consumed human flesh, and stored stolen blood. After serving 12 years, he was released in 2002.

Nicholas Lungisa Ncama

Aliases: None
DOB: 1972
Nationality: South African
Active Years: 1996–1997
Victims: 8
Location: South Africa
MO: Strangulation, stabbing
Conviction: Sentenced to life imprisonment
Brief biography:

Nicholas Lungisa Ncama was a South African serial killer active in the Eastern Cape Province. His brutal spree ended with his capture, and he was sentenced to life imprisonment.

Nicholas Trapishkin

Aliases: N/A
DOB: c. 1900
Nationality: Russian
Active Years: 1920–1926
Victims: 100 suspected
Location: Russia
MO: Strangulation, stabbing
Conviction: Death sentence, 1926
Brief biography:

Nicholas Trapishkin is alleged to have murdered over 100 people in Russia using methods of strangulation and stabbing. He was convicted by the Moscow Supreme Court and executed in 1926.

Chapter Fifteen: O-List

Ottis Elwood Toole and Henry Lee Lucas

Aliases: N/A
DOB: Toole: March 5, 1947; Lucas: August 23, 1936
Nationality: American
Active Years: 1976–1983
Victims: Suspected of 100+ combined
Location: Across the U.S.
MO: Kidnapping, rape, and murder
Conviction: Toole: Died in prison; Lucas: Life imprisonment, commuted from death sentence

Brief biography:

Ottis Toole and Henry Lee Lucas are believed to have committed over a hundred murders across the United States, though the extent of their crimes is uncertain due to their frequent lies and exaggerations. They shared a disturbing relationship, claiming to have killed together. Lucas's death sentence was later commuted to life, and Toole died in prison. Their confessions led to numerous closed cases, though their credibility remains highly debated.

Order of Assassins

Aliases: "Hashashin"
DOB: 1090
Nationality: Persian
Active Years: 1090-1256
Victims: Dozens
Location: Persia, Levant
MO: Political assassinations, stealth killings
Conviction: Dissolved by Mongols
Brief biography:

The Order of Assassins, known as the "Hashashin," was a medieval Islamic sect that operated in Persia and the Levant. Known for their stealth and skill in high-profile assassinations of political and religious leaders, they used infiltration and surprise to reach even the most fortified enemies. The Mongol Empire ultimately dissolved the group in 1256, but their mystique and influence on perceptions of covert operations and intrigue endure to this day.

Chapter Sixteen: P-List

Patrice Alegre

Aliases: None
DOB: 1968
Nationality: French
Active Years: 1990s
Victims: 5 confirmed
Location: France
MO: Strangulation
Conviction: Life imprisonment

Brief biography:

Patrice Alegre, a French serial killer, was convicted of the brutal rape and strangulation murders of five women in the 1990s. His violent crimes shocked France, as he was eventually linked to multiple unsolved cases through investigative efforts. Alegre remains in prison for life, and his case received widespread media coverage due to the cruelty of his acts.

Pedro Lopez

Aliases: The Monster of the Andes
DOB: October 8, 1948
Nationality: Colombian
Active Years: 1969–1980
Victims: 110+ confirmed
Location: Colombia, Ecuador, Peru
MO: Rape, strangulation
Conviction: Released in 1998, whereabouts unknown
Brief biography:

Pedro Lopez, also known as "The Monster of the Andes," is one of history's most prolific serial killers, confessing to over 350 murders, with 110 confirmed. His horrifying spree targeted young girls across Colombia, Ecuador, and Peru. After his release in Ecuador in 1998 for "good behavior," his whereabouts remain unknown, and many fear he may still be free.

Peter Kürten

Aliases: The Vampire of Düsseldorf
DOB: May 26, 1883
Nationality: German
Active Years: 1913–1930
Victims: Estimated 9–79
Location: Düsseldorf, Germany
MO: Stabbing, strangulation, drinking blood
Conviction: Executed by guillotine in 1931
Brief biography:

Peter Kürten, "The Vampire of Düsseldorf," spread terror across Düsseldorf with his violent crimes involving blood drinking, stabbing, and strangulation. He was executed by guillotine in 1931, leaving behind a legacy of horror in Germany.

Peter Manuel

Aliases: The Beast of Birkenshaw
DOB: March 15, 1927
Nationality: Scottish
Active Years: 1956–1958
Victims: 9 confirmed
Location: Scotland
MO: Shooting, sexual assault
Conviction: Executed by hanging in 1958
Brief biography:

Peter Manuel, "The Beast of Birkenshaw," was a notorious Scottish serial killer responsible for nine deaths. His crimes, marked by execution-style shootings, earned him infamy in Scotland. Captured after attempting to use stolen cash, Manuel confessed and was sentenced to hang.

Peter Tobin

Aliases: Pat McLaughlin
DOB: August 27, 1946
Nationality: Scottish
Active Years: 1991–2006
Victims: 3 confirmed, suspected 48+
Location: Scotland, England
MO: Sexual assault, stabbing, strangulation
Conviction: Life imprisonment without parole
Brief biography:

Scottish killer Peter Tobin was convicted of three murders and is suspected of many more, possibly connected to the unidentified "Bible John." His victims were brutally murdered and hidden, and he remains imprisoned for life.

Peter Sutcliffe

Aliases: The Yorkshire Ripper
DOB: June 2, 1946
Nationality: British
Active Years: 1975–1980
Victims: 13 confirmed
Location: Yorkshire, England
MO: Hammer attacks, stabbing
Conviction: Life imprisonment; died in 2020
Brief biography:

Peter Sutcliffe, the Yorkshire Ripper, targeted women in Yorkshire, violently attacking them with a hammer and stabbing them. After years of evading capture, he was arrested in 1981. Sutcliffe died in 2020 while serving life in prison.

Petr Zelenka

Aliases: None
DOB: February 27, 1976
Nationality: Czech
Active Years: 2006
Victims: 7 murdered, 10 attempted
Location: Havlickuv Brod, Czech Republic
MO: Poisoning patients with heparin

Conviction: Sentenced to life in 2008
Brief biography:

Petr Zelenka, a Czech nurse, poisoned seven patients and attempted to kill ten others with lethal doses of heparin. His crimes led to a life sentence in 2008.

Philipp Tyurin

Aliases: None
DOB: 1910
Nationality: Russian
Active Years: 1945–1946
Victims: Estimated 29
Location: Leningrad, USSR
MO: Lured victims, killed with heavy objects
Conviction: Executed by firing squad in 1947
Brief biography:

Philipp Tyurin murdered nearly 30 people in Leningrad post-WWII, killing victims he lured with trade offers. He was sentenced to death and executed in 1947.

Pierre Voirbo

Aliases: None
DOB: c. 1835
Nationality: French
Active Years: 1860s
Victims: 10
Location: Paris, France
MO: Murdering creditors and robbery victims
Conviction: Committed suicide before trial in 1869
Brief biography:

Pierre Voirbo, a Parisian police officer, was suspected of murdering at least ten people, including creditors and robbery victims. Though he confessed to one murder, he committed suicide before facing trial in 1869.

Chapter Seventeen: R-List

Ralph Raymond Andrews

Aliases: None
DOB: 1938
Nationality: American
Active Years: 1973-1975
Victims: 4
Location: Texas, USA
MO: Strangulation, robbery
Conviction: Life in prison

Brief biography:

Ralph Raymond Andrews, a Texas native, murdered four women during a robbery spree in the 1970s, strangling each after robbing them. Known for his violent tendencies, Andrews was eventually identified by a surviving victim. He was sentenced to life imprisonment, where he remains to this day.

Rahway Jane Doe

Aliases: None
DOB: Unknown
Nationality: -
Active Years: 1887
Victims: 1
Location: Rahway, New Jersey, USA
MO: Throat slashed, blunt force trauma
Conviction: Unsolved
Brief biography:

In 1887, the body of an unidentified young woman was discovered in Rahway, New Jersey. Brutally beaten and her throat slashed, this unsolved case, nicknamed Rahway Jane Doe, remains shrouded in mystery. Suspicions have linked it to Jack the Ripper theories, but her true identity and the killer remain unknown.

Randy Kraft

Aliases: The Scorecard Killer
DOB: March 19, 1945
Nationality: American
Active Years: 1971–1983
Victims: 16 confirmed, possibly 60+
Location: USA
MO: Torture, strangulation, sexual assault
Conviction: Sentenced to death (1989)
Brief biography:

Known as "The Scorecard Killer," Randy Kraft kept a coded list of his victims, primarily young men he tortured and murdered. Arrested in 1983, Kraft was found with a dead Marine in his car, leading to his conviction. Authorities suspect him in over 60 murders. He remains on death row.

Ramiro Artieda

Aliases: None
DOB: 1950
Nationality: Bolivian
Active Years: 1980s-1990s
Victims: 5+
Location: Bolivia
MO: Poisoning, strangulation
Conviction: Life imprisonment
Brief biography:

Ramiro Artieda, a Bolivian serial killer, poisoned and strangled at least five victims, including two wives. He was elusive for a decade, finally apprehended in the 1990s. Known for his chilling demeanor, Artieda is serving a life sentence in Bolivia.

Ray and Faye Copeland

Aliases: None
DOB: Ray: Dec 30, 1914; Faye: Aug 4, 1921

Nationality: American
Active Years: 1986–1989
Victims: 5 confirmed
Location: Missouri, USA
MO: Lured drifters, killed them
Conviction: Ray: Death; Faye: Life (commuted from death)
Brief biography:

The oldest couple sentenced to death in the U.S., Ray and Faye Copeland lured drifters to work on their farm, later killing them. Ray died in prison, and Faye's sentence was commuted to life, where she later died.

Raya and Sakina

Aliases: None
DOB: Unknown
Nationality: Egyptian
Active Years: 1919–1920
Victims: Estimated 17
Location: Alexandria, Egypt
MO: Lured women, suffocated them, stole jewelry
Conviction: Executed in 1921
Brief biography:

Sisters Raya and Sakina were the first Egyptian women executed for murder, responsible for luring and killing at least 17 women for their jewelry. Their crimes shocked Egypt, and their execution marked a historic moment in Egyptian criminal justice.

Richard Allen Williams

Aliases: None
DOB: 1966
Nationality: American
Active Years: 1993–1994
Victims: 10 suspected
Location: Missouri, USA
MO: Lethal drug administration

Conviction: Released due to prosecutorial errors
Brief biography:

Williams, a nurse at Truman Veterans Hospital, allegedly killed 10 patients with the drug succinylcholine. Due to forensic errors, he was released without formal charges. His case remains controversial and unresolved.

Richard Arinaitwe

Aliases: None
DOB: 1974
Nationality: Ugandan
Active Years: 1990s-2000s
Victims: 3+
Location: Kampala, Uganda
MO: Stabbing, mutilation
Conviction: Life imprisonment
Brief biography:

Ugandan serial killer Richard Arinaitwe, responsible for at least three murders, including a prominent lawyer, gained notoriety for his cold, brutal methods. He continues to serve a life sentence and remains known for his defiant behavior in court.

Richard Cottingham

Aliases: The Torso Killer, The New York Ripper
DOB: Nov 25, 1946
Nationality: American
Active Years: 1967–1980
Victims: 11 confirmed, suspected of more
Location: New Jersey, New York
MO: Torture, sexual assault, dismemberment
Conviction: Life imprisonment (multiple life sentences)
Brief biography:

Richard Cottingham earned his nickname "The Torso Killer" for dismembering his victims and often leaving only their torsos behind. His brutal killings shocked New

York and New Jersey until his 1980 arrest. He is serving multiple life sentences for his crimes.

Richard Fran Biegenwald

Aliases: Thrill Killer
DOB: Aug 24, 1940
Nationality: American
Active Years: 1958–1983
Victims: 5 confirmed
Location: New Jersey, USA
MO: Shooting victims, burying bodies
Conviction: Four life sentences, died in 2008
Brief biography:

The "Thrill Killer" Richard Fran Biegenwald murdered at least five people, driven by a fascination with violence. His death sentence was commuted to four life terms, and he spent his final years in prison until his death in 2008.

Richard Lee Tingler Jr.

Aliases: None
DOB: December 1940
Nationality: American
Active Years: 1961–1968
Victims: 6 confirmed
Location: Ohio, USA
MO: Shot victims, robbery
Conviction: Death penalty, commuted to life (1969)
Brief biography:

Richard Lee Tingler Jr., a career criminal, killed six people during a string of violent robberies in Ohio during the 1960s. Known for his brutal methods, including shooting victims, Tingler's death sentence was later commuted to life imprisonment in 1969.

Richard Ramirez

Aliases: The Night Stalker
DOB: February 29, 1960
Nationality: American
Active Years: 1984–1985
Victims: 14 confirmed, suspected 16+
Location: California, primarily Los Angeles
MO: Home invasions, sexual assaults, murder by gun and knife
Conviction: Sentenced to death in 1989, died of cancer in 2013
Brief biography:

Richard Ramirez terrorized Los Angeles with a spree of home invasions, assaults, and murders over a two-year period. Known for his brutality and satanic influences, he was captured by civilians after a failed carjacking and sentenced to death. He died in 2013 while awaiting execution.

Richard Trenton Chase

Aliases: The Vampire of Sacramento
DOB: May 23, 1950
Nationality: American
Active Years: 1977-1978
Victims: 6
Location: Sacramento, California
MO: Cannibalism, blood-drinking, necrophilia
Conviction: Sentenced to death, committed suicide in 1980
Brief biography:

Richard Chase, known for his horrific acts of cannibalism and blood-drinking, killed six people in Sacramento. He believed consuming blood would prevent his own death, a result of severe mental illness. He committed suicide in prison shortly after his sentencing.

Robert Ben Rhoades

Aliases: Truck Stop Killer
DOB: November 22, 1945
Nationality: American
Active Years: 1975–1990
Victims: 3 confirmed, suspected 50+

Location: Multiple states, USA
MO: Abduction, torture, sexual assault, murder
Conviction: Life imprisonment without parole (1994)
Brief biography:

Known as the Truck Stop Killer, Robert Rhoades is suspected of murdering over 50 victims. His truck served as a mobile torture chamber, where he preyed on hitchhikers. He was apprehended after a victim escaped and sentenced to life without parole in 1994.

Roger Andermatt

Aliases: The Death Nurse
DOB: 1969
Nationality: Swiss
Active Years: 1995-2001
Victims: 22 confirmed
Location: Switzerland
MO: Overdosing patients
Conviction: Life imprisonment
Brief biography:

Roger Andermatt, a Swiss nurse, murdered 22 elderly patients in nursing homes by administering lethal doses of drugs. While he claimed to be ending their suffering, the systematic nature of his crimes led to his conviction and life sentence.

Robert Arguelles

Aliases: None
DOB: 1957
Nationality: American
Active Years: 1992-1996
Victims: 4
Location: Utah, USA
MO: Kidnapping, sexual assault, stabbing
Conviction: Sentenced to death
Brief biography:

Robert Arguelles, a Utah serial killer, targeted vulnerable women in a series of brutal attacks involving kidnapping, rape, and murder. His confessions and evidence led to a death sentence, though he died of natural causes before his execution.

Robert Clive Napper

Aliases: None
DOB: 1966
Nationality: British
Active Years: 1992–1993
Victims: 3
Location: London, England
MO: Rape, stabbing
Conviction: Indefinite imprisonment
Brief biography:

Robert Clive Napper, a convicted serial killer and rapist, committed multiple violent assaults in the UK, including the high-profile murder of Rachel Nickell. Diagnosed with paranoid schizophrenia, Napper remains confined to a psychiatric hospital.

Robert Sylvester Alston

Aliases: None
DOB: 1960
Nationality: American
Active Years: 1980s-1990s
Victims: 4 confirmed
Location: New York, USA
MO: Rape, strangulation
Conviction: Life imprisonment
Brief biography:

Alston was convicted of murdering and assaulting women in New York. He targeted vulnerable women, luring them to isolated areas before attacking. Arrested in 1993, he is serving a life sentence without parole.

Robison Family Murders

Aliases: None
DOB: Various
Nationality: American
Active Years: 1968
Victims: 6
Location: Good Hart, Michigan, USA
MO: Shooting, bludgeoning
Conviction: Unsolved (primary suspect Joseph Scolaro III committed suicide)
Brief biography:

In 1968, the Robison family was found murdered in their vacation home. Suspicions fell on business associate Joseph Scolaro, who later committed suicide, leaving a note claiming innocence. The case remains unsolved.

Robert Leroy Anderson

Aliases: None
DOB: 1969
Nationality: American
Active Years: 1994-1997
Victims: 2 confirmed
Location: South Dakota, USA
MO: Kidnapping, sexual assault, strangulation
Conviction: Death penalty (executed in 2003)
Brief biography:

Known for his meticulous planning, Anderson was convicted of the abduction and murder of two women in South Dakota. Captured after evidence linked him to the crimes, he was sentenced to death and executed in 2003.

Robert Simon (Mudman)

Aliases: Mudman
DOB: 1954
Nationality: American
Active Years: 1975–1995
Victims: 8

Location: New Jersey/Pennsylvania, USA
MO: Shooting and assault
Conviction: Executed in 1995
Brief biography:

Robert "Mudman" Simon, a motorcycle gang member, was convicted of eight murders. His violent spree lasted over two decades, marked by brutal shootings and assaults. After committing a murder while on parole, he was sentenced to death and executed in 1995.

Rodney James Alcala (The Dating Game Killer)

Aliases: The Dating Game Killer
DOB: 1943
Nationality: American
Active Years: 1970s-1980s
Victims: 8+ confirmed
Location: California, USA
MO: Rape, torture, and strangulation
Conviction: Sentenced to death, died in 2021
Brief biography:

Rodney Alcala, infamously known for his appearance on "The Dating Game," lured victims with his charm and photography skills before subjecting them to horrific torture and murder. Though convicted of eight murders, authorities suspect more victims remain unidentified. He was sentenced to death in 2010 but died of natural causes in 2021 while on death row.

Room 1046 - Roland T. Owen (Artemus Ogletree)

Aliases: None
DOB: Unknown
Nationality: American
Active Years: 1935
Victims: 1 (Owen/Artemus Ogletree)
Location: Hotel President, Kansas City
MO: Tied, stabbed, and left to die
Conviction: Unsolved
Brief biography:

In 1935, Roland T. Owen (later identified as Artemus Ogletree) was found bound and fatally stabbed in Room 1046 at the Hotel President in Kansas City. Despite briefly speaking to investigators, he could not identify his assailant, and his case remains one of the city's enduring unsolved mysteries.

Ronald Allridge and James Allridge III

Aliases: None
DOB: Ronald: October 8, 1963; James: November 18, 1962
Nationality: American
Active Years: 1980s
Victims: 3 confirmed
Location: Fort Worth, Texas
MO: Armed robbery, shooting
Conviction: Executed (Ronald: 1995; James: 2004)
Brief biography:

Brothers Ronald and James Allridge III committed a series of violent robberies and murders in Texas in the 1980s. Both were sentenced to death for their crimes, with Ronald executed in 1995 and James in 2004. James expressed remorse before his execution.

Rodney Alcala (The Dating Game Killer)

Aliases: The Dating Game Killer
DOB: August 23, 1943
Nationality: American
Active Years: 1968–1979
Victims: 5+ (convicted)
Location: United States
MO: Strangulation, sexual assault
Conviction: Sentenced to death multiple times
Brief biography:

Rodney Alcala, often remembered for his charm on a dating show, lured victims by posing as a photographer. His series of murders spanned from the late 1960s to the

1970s. Convicted of five murders, authorities suspect he may have more victims. He remained on death row until his death in 2021.

Rory Enrique Conde (Tamiami Strangler)

Aliases: Tamiami Strangler
DOB: June 14, 1965
Nationality: Colombian
Active Years: 1994–1995
Victims: 6
Location: Miami, Florida, USA
MO: Strangled and murdered prostitutes
Conviction: Sentenced to death, 5 life sentences
Brief biography:

Rory Conde murdered six women in Miami, Florida, between 1994 and 1995. Known as the Tamiami Strangler, he targeted prostitutes, leaving messages on their bodies. He was arrested and sentenced to death, along with five life terms.

Russell Dermond

Aliases: None
DOB: December 10, 1925
Nationality: American
Active Years: 2014
Victims: 2 (Russell and Shirley Dermond)
Location: Lake Oconee, Georgia, USA
MO: Beheading (Russell); drowning (Shirley)
Conviction: Unsolved
Brief biography:

Russell Dermond was found beheaded in his garage, while his wife, Shirley, was discovered in Lake Oconee days later. Despite extensive investigation, no suspects have been identified, and the case remains unsolved, with the motive still unknown.

Chapter Eighteen: S-List

Saeed Hanaei

Aliases: None
DOB: 1962
Nationality: Iranian
Active Years: 2000–2001
Victims: 16
Location: Iran
MO: Strangulation with victims' headscarves
Conviction: Hanged, 2002

Brief biography:

Saeed Hanaei murdered 16 prostitutes in Mashhad, Iran, claiming a religious motive. Initially praised by some extremists, his abuse of victims prior to their deaths was later uncovered. Hanaei was executed in 2002.

Sarah and John Makin

Aliases: None
DOB: Sarah: 1845; John: 1840
Nationality: Australian
Active Years: 1890s
Victims: 12 confirmed
Location: Sydney, Australia
MO: Baby farming, neglect, and murder of infants
Conviction: John was hanged in 1893, Sarah's sentence commuted to life
Brief biography:

The Makins profited from taking in illegitimate infants, only to neglect and kill them. After remains were found across their rented properties, John was hanged, and Sarah's sentence was reduced to life.

Seisaku Nakamura

Aliases: None
DOB: 1924
Nationality: Japanese
Active Years: 1938–1942
Victims: 4
Location: Japan
MO: Strangulation, stabbing
Conviction: Executed in 1943
Brief biography:

Nakamura targeted young girls in Japan, often strangling and consuming parts of their bodies. He was captured and executed in 1943, his crimes marking a disturbing period in Japanese criminal history.

Serhiy Tkach

Aliases: None
DOB: September 12, 1952
Nationality: Ukrainian
Active Years: 1984–2005
Victims: 36 confirmed, 100+ claimed
Location: Ukraine
MO: Suffocation, necrophilia
Conviction: Life imprisonment, died in 2018
Brief biography:

Tkach, a former police investigator, murdered girls and young women over two decades, performing sexual acts on their corpses. Convicted for 36 murders, he claimed over 100 victims and died in prison in 2018.

Servant Girl Annihilator

Aliases: None
DOB: Unknown

Nationality: American
Active Years: 1884–1885
Victims: 7+
Location: Austin, Texas, USA
MO: Attacked with an axe
Conviction: Unsolved
Brief biography:

The Annihilator killed at least seven people in Austin, Texas, by attacking them with an axe. Despite multiple suspects, the killer's identity remains a mystery, and the murders abruptly stopped.

Stanislaw Modzelewski (Vampire of Galkowek)

Aliases: The Vampire of Galkowek
DOB: March 15, 1929
Nationality: Polish
Active Years: 1952–1967
Victims: 7-8 victims, 6 attempts
Location: Poland
MO: Strangulation, sexual assault
Conviction: Executed in 1959
Brief biography:

Known for brutal murders of women, Modzelewski was caught after a string of strangulations and assaults. He was sentenced to death and hanged in 1959.

Steven Gordon and Franc Cano

Aliases: None
DOB: Unknown
Nationality: American
Active Years: 2013–2014
Victims: 4 confirmed
Location: Orange County, California
MO: Abduction, rape, murder
Conviction: Death sentence
Brief biography:

Despite GPS monitoring, Gordon and Cano, registered sex offenders, managed to kidnap, rape, and kill four women in Orange County, CA. They were eventually convicted and sentenced to death.

Stephen Akinmurele (The Cul-De-Sac Killer)

Aliases: The Cul-De-Sac Killer
DOB: 1978
Nationality: British
Active Years: 1995–1998
Victims: 5 confirmed
Location: England
MO: Strangulation, arson
Conviction: Died by suicide before trial
Brief biography:

Akinmurele targeted elderly victims in England, strangling them and setting fires. He died by suicide before facing trial, leaving behind a trail of horrific crimes targeting the vulnerable.

Stephen D. Richards (Nebraska Fiend)

Aliases: Nebraska Fiend
DOB: 1856
Nationality: American
Active Years: 1879
Victims: 9
Location: Nebraska, USA
MO: Bludgeoning, shooting
Conviction: Executed in 1879
Brief biography:

Richards murdered nine people, including women and children, in Nebraska. Known for his brutality, he was quickly caught, tried, and hanged in the same year, his case shocking the public.

Springfield Three

Aliases: None
DOB: Various
Nationality: American
Active Years: 1992
Victims: 3 (disappeared)
Location: Springfield, Missouri, USA
MO: Disappearance
Conviction: Unsolved
Brief biography:

Sherill Levitt, her daughter Suzanne Streeter, and friend Stacy McCall vanished from their Springfield home in 1992. With no bodies and few clues, the case remains one of America's most baffling missing persons cases.

Sodder Children

Aliases: None
DOB: Various
Nationality: American
Active Years: 1945
Victims: 5 (disappeared)
Location: Fayetteville, West Virginia, USA
MO: Disappearance, suspected kidnapping or death
Conviction: Unsolved; no remains found, possible abduction theories
Brief biography:

On Christmas Eve 1945, five Sodder children vanished after a fire destroyed their home. Though five family members escaped, the missing children's bodies were never recovered. Multiple eyewitness reports suggested sightings of the children afterward, leading their parents to suspect abduction. Despite extensive investigations, the mystery remains unsolved.

Sophie Charlotte Elizabeth Ursinus

Aliases: None
DOB: May 5, 1760
Nationality: Prussian

Active Years: 1800–1801
Victims: 2 confirmed, more suspected
Location: Prussia (now Poland)
MO: Poisoning with arsenic
Conviction: Sentenced to life in prison, pardoned in 1833
Brief biography:

Sophie Ursinus, a Prussian noblewoman, poisoned her husband and aunt in the early 1800s. After a servant survived her arsenic poisoning attempt, authorities investigated, confirming the deaths of two victims and suspecting her involvement in more. Ursinus served life in prison but was pardoned in 1833, living the rest of her life in upper-class society until her death in 1836.

Süleyman Aktaş (Nailing Killer)

Aliases: Nailing Killer
DOB: 1943
Nationality: Turkish
Active Years: 1986, 1994
Victims: 5
Location: Turkey
MO: Driving nails into victims' heads
Conviction: Sentenced to life imprisonment
Brief biography:

Known as the "Nailing Killer," Süleyman Aktaş terrorized Turkey by driving nails into the skulls of his victims in 1986 and 1994. Diagnosed with schizophrenia, he still faced conviction, receiving a life sentence. His chilling methods and psychotic tendencies solidify his place as one of Turkey's most infamous criminals.

Chapter Nineteen: T-List

Takahiro Shiraishi

Aliases: Zama Suicide Pact Killer / Twitter Killer
DOB: 1991
Nationality: Japanese
Active Years: 2017
Victims: 9 murdered
Location: Zama, Japan
MO: Lured victims through Twitter, strangled and dismembered them
Conviction: Sentenced to death in 2020

Brief biography:

Takahiro Shiraishi, also known as the "Twitter Killer," murdered nine individuals he met through a site for those contemplating suicide. Between August and October 2017, he lured them to his apartment, strangled, and dismembered them. Shiraishi was arrested in October 2017 after body parts were found in his home and was sentenced to death in 2020.

Tammy Corrine Terrell

Aliases: None
DOB: 1963
Nationality: American
Active Years: 1980
Victims: 1 (Tammy Terrell)
Location: Roswell, New Mexico
MO: Beaten with a hammer, stabbed, sexually assaulted
Conviction: Unsolved
Brief biography:

Tammy Corrine Terrell's body was found in 1980 near Roswell, New Mexico. With severe wounds suggesting brutal assault, she remained unidentified until 2021 when forensic genealogy linked her to her family. Her murder remains unsolved.

Tara Calico

Aliases: None
DOB: February 28, 1969
Nationality: American
Active Years: 1988
Victims: 1 (disappeared)
Location: Belen, New Mexico, USA
MO: Likely abduction, possible Polaroid of bound woman resembling Tara
Conviction: Unsolved
Brief biography:

Tara Calico disappeared while biking near her home in 1988. Witnesses reported seeing a suspicious vehicle, but she was never found. A year later, a Polaroid surfaced showing a bound woman resembling Tara, fueling theories of abduction. Authorities are still investigating, but no arrests have been made.

Ted Bundy

Aliases: None
DOB: November 24, 1946
Nationality: American
Active Years: 1974–1978
Victims: 30+ confirmed
Location: Multiple states across the USA
MO: Lured women, sexually assaulted, bludgeoned, strangled
Conviction: Executed by electric chair (1989)

Brief biography:

Ted Bundy, one of America's most infamous serial killers, lured and murdered over 30 women across several states in the 1970s. Known for his charm, Bundy feigned injury or posed as an authority to gain trust before assaulting and killing his victims. Captured after escaping custody twice, Bundy was executed in 1989, his story continuing to captivate public interest.

The Alligator Man (Joe Ball)

Aliases: None
DOB: 1896
Nationality: American
Active Years: 1930s
Victims: 20+ suspected
Location: Texas, USA
MO: Shot victims, fed bodies to alligators
Conviction: Suicide (no trial)
Brief biography:

Joe Ball, "The Alligator Man," ran a Texas tavern in the 1930s and allegedly murdered over 20 women, disposing of their bodies by feeding them to alligators. When police closed in on him, Ball took his own life, leaving many questions about his total victim count unanswered.

The Axeman of New Orleans

Aliases: The Axeman
DOB: Unknown
Nationality: American
Active Years: 1918–1919
Victims: 6 confirmed, 12 attacked
Location: New Orleans, LA
MO: Attacked victims with an ax found at the scene
Conviction: Unsolved
Brief biography:

The Axeman terrorized New Orleans between 1918 and 1919, killing six and injuring many more. He famously wrote a letter declaring that anyone playing jazz music would be spared. His identity was never discovered, and his attacks stopped as mysteriously as they began.

The Boston Strangler (Albert DeSalvo)

Aliases: The Boston Strangler
DOB: September 3, 1931
Nationality: American

Active Years: 1962–1964
Victims: 13
Location: Boston, Massachusetts
MO: Strangulation after sexual assault
Conviction: Confessed but never convicted for the murders
Brief biography:

Albert DeSalvo confessed to being the Boston Strangler, responsible for the brutal murders of 13 women between 1962 and 1964. Though linked by DNA to one victim, DeSalvo was never formally tried for these murders, leaving some questions about his culpability.

The Colony of Roanoke

Aliases: Lost Colony
DOB: 1587
Nationality: British
Active Years: 1587
Victims: Estimated 115 people
Location: Roanoke Island
MO: Entire colony disappeared without a trace
Conviction: Unsolved
Brief biography:

The Roanoke Colony vanished between 1587 and 1590, leaving only the word "Croatoan" carved into a tree. Theories about their fate range from integration with local tribes to a violent demise, but the mystery of Roanoke remains unsolved.

The Doodler

Aliases: The Doodler
DOB: Unknown
Nationality: Unknown
Active Years: 1974–1975
Victims: 6–16
Location: San Francisco, California
MO: Sketched victims, then stabbed them to death
Conviction: Unsolved
Brief biography:

The Doodler targeted San Francisco's gay community in the mid-1970s, sketching his victims before killing them. Though three survivors refused to testify, advancements in DNA may offer new clues to this unsolved case.

The Grimes Sisters (Patricia and Barbara)

Aliases: None
DOB: Patricia: 1941; Barbara: 1944
Nationality: American
Active Years: 1956
Victims: 2
Location: Chicago, Illinois, USA
MO: Possible abduction, cause of death uncertain
Conviction: Unsolved
Brief biography:

Patricia and Barbara Grimes disappeared in 1956 after attending a movie. Their bodies were found a month later, with the cause of death remaining unclear. Despite sightings and multiple leads, their deaths remain one of Chicago's oldest unsolved mysteries.

Theodore "Ted" Kaczynski (The Unabomber)

Aliases: The Unabomber
DOB: May 22, 1942
Nationality: American
Active Years: 1978–1995
Victims: 3 murdered, 23 injured
Location: USA (Various states)
MO: Sent mail bombs to universities and airlines
Conviction: Sentenced to life in prison, 1998
Brief biography:

Theodore "Ted" Kaczynski, a former Harvard-educated mathematician, turned domestic terrorist, conducted a bombing campaign to protest against modern technology, which he believed was eroding human freedom. Kaczynski was arrested in 1996 after his brother recognized his writing style in a manifesto published by the FBI. His case brought national attention to issues of privacy and surveillance.

The Isdal Woman

Aliases: The Isdal Woman
DOB: Unknown
Nationality: Unknown
Active Years: 1970
Victims: 1
Location: Isdalen Valley, Norway
MO: Found burned, identity concealed
Conviction: Unsolved
Brief biography:

The Isdal Woman was discovered burned to death in Norway's Isdalen Valley in 1970. Evidence suggested she took extreme measures to conceal her identity, as labels were removed from her belongings, and her fingerprints were altered. With links to espionage theories, her true identity and the circumstances surrounding her death remain one of Norway's most enduring mysteries.

Tony Abels

Aliases: None
DOB: 1963
Nationality: American
Active Years: 1980s
Victims: 3 confirmed
Location: Florida, USA
MO: Stabbings
Conviction: Life imprisonment
Brief biography:

Tony Abels was convicted of murdering three women in Florida in the 1980s. Using DNA evidence, police were able to link Abels to his victims, whom he lured into secluded areas before killing. He received a life sentence without parole.

Terry Samuel Arnold

Aliases: None
DOB: 1965
Nationality: Canadian
Active Years: 1980s–1990s
Victims: 1+
Location: Canada
MO: Sexual assault, bludgeoning
Conviction: Died by suicide awaiting trial
Brief biography:

Terry Samuel Arnold, a suspected serial killer and sex offender from Canada, was linked to multiple unsolved cases, including the wrongful conviction of another man for Christine Jessop's murder. Arnold committed suicide in 2005, leaving many unresolved questions and lingering suspicions about additional crimes.

Thomas Griffiths Wainewright

Aliases: None
DOB: October 1794
Nationality: British
Active Years: 1830s
Victims: 5 suspected
Location: London, England
MO: Poisoned with strychnine
Conviction: Sentenced to penal colony, died in 1847
Brief biography:

Thomas Griffiths Wainewright, a writer and artist, poisoned multiple family members with strychnine for financial gain. Sentenced to a penal colony in Tasmania, he continued his artistry until his death. His crimes, steeped in Victorian scandal, made him infamous in 19th-century Britain.

Thomas Quick (Sattermannen)

Aliases: Sattermannen (The Sandman)
DOB: 1950
Nationality: Swedish
Active Years: 1990–1994
Victims: 8

Location: Sweden
MO: Sexual assault and stabbing
Conviction: Confessions later recanted, no convictions
Brief biography:

Thomas Quick, born Sture Bergwall, confessed to more than 30 murders, only to later retract his statements, leading to his acquittal. His case exposed serious flaws in Sweden's justice system and highlighted the dangers of coercive interrogations and false confessions.

Thomas Warren Whisenhant

Aliases: None
DOB: January 29, 1947
Nationality: American
Active Years: 1970s
Victims: 3 known victims
Location: Mobile County, Alabama
MO: Abduction, rape, murder, body mutilation
Conviction: Executed by lethal injection in 2010
Brief biography:

Thomas Warren Whisenhant abducted and murdered women, returning to mutilate the bodies. Arrested near a crime scene, Whisenhant's long legal battle ended in execution in 2010, leaving a legacy of terror and a complex legal case in Alabama's criminal history.

Tylenol Murders

Aliases: None
DOB: N/A
Nationality: American
Active Years: 1982
Victims: 7
Location: Chicago, IL
MO: Cyanide-laced Tylenol capsules
Conviction: No conviction for murders, James Lewis convicted of extortion
Brief biography:

In 1982, the Chicago Tylenol Murders shook the nation when cyanide-laced capsules killed seven people, prompting a nationwide recall. James Lewis, a suspect, was convicted of extortion but not linked to the murders. The case remains unsolved, though it led to reforms in packaging and product safety.

The Zodiac Killer

Aliases: The Zodiac Killer
DOB: Unknown
Nationality: American
Active Years: 1968–1969
Victims: 5 confirmed, claims 37
Location: San Francisco, CA
MO: Shooting, stabbing, taunting authorities
Conviction: Unsolved
Brief biography:

The Zodiac Killer, infamous for his cryptic letters and taunting behavior, claimed responsibility for 37 murders, though only five have been verified. His letters, ciphers, and the mystery of his identity have kept the case in the public eye as one of America's most infamous unsolved mysteries.

Thug Behram (Thuggee Cult Leader)

Aliases: Thuggee Cult Leader
DOB: c. 1765
Nationality: Indian
Active Years: 1790s–1840
Victims: 931 suspected
Location: Northern and Central India
MO: Strangulation using a ceremonial cloth (rumal)
Conviction: Executed by hanging, 1840
Brief biography:

Thug Behram led the notorious Thuggee cult in India, claiming to have strangled hundreds of travelers using a ceremonial cloth, known as a rumal. Although he admitted to only 125 murders, British authorities suspected his involvement in nearly 1,000 deaths, leading to his execution in 1840. His case remains one of the darkest chapters in India's history of organized crime.

Tony Vick

Aliases: None
DOB: April 3, 1962
Nationality: American
Active Years: 1993-1996
Victims: 4
Location: Tennessee, USA
MO: Murdered for insurance money
Conviction: Life imprisonment, serving sentence in Tennessee

Brief biography:

Tony Vick, a Tennessee native, committed four murders between 1993 and 1996, targeting his wife, fiancée, and two additional victims to collect insurance payouts. Convicted in 1997 and 1998, he received a life sentence. While in prison, Vick authored *Secrets From a Prison Cell*, where he details his experiences of life behind bars. His story serves as a chilling example of greed-fueled violence and betrayal.

Chapter Twenty: V-List

Valery Asratyan

Aliases: None
DOB: 1949
Nationality: Russian
Active Years: 1990s
Victims: 7
Location: Moscow, Russia
MO: Strangulation, sexual assault
Conviction: Life in prison

Brief biography:

Valery Asratyan, a former doctor, became one of Russia's most notorious serial killers, murdering seven women in Moscow during the 1990s. Luring his victims under the pretense of providing medical assistance, Asratyan would strangle and sexually assault them. His high-profile background added to the shock of his crimes. He was arrested, convicted, and sentenced to life imprisonment.

Vasile Tcaciuc

Aliases: The Butcher of Iasi
DOB: c. 1900
Nationality: Romanian
Active Years: Early 1930s
Victims: 21–27
Location: Iasi, Romania
MO: Lured victims to woods, killed with an axe
Conviction: Shot dead while trying to escape
Brief biography:

Vasile Tcaciuc, known as the Butcher of Iasi, was a Romanian serial killer active in the 1930s. He and his girlfriend lured victims into the woods, where he murdered them with an axe. Tcaciuc's reign of terror ended in 1935 when police discovered human remains on his property. During a subsequent escape attempt, he was shot dead by police.

Velaphi Ndlangamandla

Aliases: None
DOB: 1962
Nationality: South African
Active Years: 1998
Victims: 19
Location: Mpumalanga, South Africa
MO: Strangulation, bludgeoning
Conviction: Sentenced to life imprisonment
Brief biography:

Velaphi Ndlangamandla was a South African serial killer who murdered 19 people in Mpumalanga in 1998. His victims were bludgeoned and strangled, leaving a horrific impact on the region. Ndlangamandla was captured and sentenced to life imprisonment, his crimes leaving a lasting mark on South Africa's criminal history.

Vladimir Mukhankin

Aliases: None
DOB: 1960
Nationality: Russian
Active Years: 1995
Victims: 8
Location: Southern Russia
MO: Murder and mutilation
Conviction: Life imprisonment
Brief biography:

Vladimir Mukhankin committed a spree of eight murders in southern Russia in 1995, targeting mostly women. His crimes were characterized by extreme violence and mutilation. Mukhankin's rampage ended with his arrest, and he was sentenced to life in prison, where he remains.

Vickie Dawn Jackson

Aliases: Angel of Death
DOB: February 13, 1966
Nationality: American
Active Years: 2000
Victims: 10+ confirmed
Location: United States
MO: Poisoning with Mivacron (a paralyzing drug)
Conviction: Sentenced to life in prison, 2006
Brief biography:

Vickie Dawn Jackson, a Texas nurse known as the "Angel of Death," killed at least 10 patients in 2000 by injecting them with a paralytic agent, Mivacron. Her victims were primarily elderly patients. She was sentenced to life in prison in 2006, leaving a chilling legacy as a healthcare worker who preyed on the vulnerable.

Villisca Axe Murders

Aliases: None
DOB: -
Nationality: -
Active Years: 1912
Victims: 8
Location: Villisca, Iowa, USA
MO: Bludgeoning with an axe
Conviction: Unsolved
Brief biography:

In 1912, eight people, including six members of the Moore family, were brutally murdered in their home in Villisca, Iowa. All victims were killed with an axe while they slept. Despite a thorough investigation and numerous suspects, the case remains unsolved and is one of America's most notorious cold cases.

Vincenzo Aiutino

Aliases: None
DOB: 1969
Nationality: Italian
Active Years: 1990s
Victims: 4 confirmed

Location: France, Italy
MO: Rape and strangulation
Conviction: Sentenced to life
Brief biography:

Vincenzo Aiutino, an Italian-born serial killer, murdered four women across France and Italy in the 1990s. His crimes involved rape followed by strangulation. DNA evidence eventually linked Aiutino to his crimes, leading to a life sentence in France, where he primarily operated.

Vincenzo Verzeni

Aliases: The Vampire of Bergamo
DOB: April 11, 1849
Nationality: Italian
Active Years: 1870–1872
Victims: 2 confirmed, suspected more
Location: Bergamo, Italy
MO: Strangled victims, drank their blood, mutilated bodies
Conviction: Sentenced to life in a mental institution, died in 1874
Brief biography:

Known as the Vampire of Bergamo, Vincenzo Verzeni strangled and mutilated two women, drinking their blood and disemboweling them. He claimed to be driven by dark urges, and after his arrest, Verzeni was sentenced to life in a mental institution, where he later took his own life in 1874. His horrific crimes have left a macabre legacy in Italian criminal history.

Volga Maniac

Active Years: 2011-2012
Victims: 32 known murders
Location: Various regions in Russia
MO: Strangulation, robbery

Details: The Volga Maniac is linked to a series of murders targeting elderly women aged 75 to 90, all living in low-cost apartments known as khrushchyovkas. The killer gained entry by posing as a social services worker or an HOA employee. The murders began in Kazan, where nine victims were reported. The killings spread to other cities, and the last three were in Ufa in September 2012. A suspect was caught on security camera footage, but the investigation remains open, with a reward of three million rubles for information. Pavel Shayakhmetov was arrested in 2017 for two murders and later committed suicide in 2018 before facing trial.

Chapter Twenty-One: W-List

Wang Fang

Aliases: None
DOB: c. 1966
Nationality: Chinese
Active Years: Unknown
Victims: 8 confirmed
Location: Henan Province, China
MO: Poisoned family members using rat poison
Conviction: Sentenced to death

Brief biography:

Wang Fang, a Chinese serial killer, murdered at least eight family members by poisoning them with "dushuqiang," a potent rat poison. Her motives stemmed from petty family disputes, and she attempted to poison additional family members. Wang was sentenced to death for her crimes in Henan Province.

Wang Qiang

Aliases: None
DOB: January 15, 1975
Nationality: Chinese
Active Years: 1995–2003
Victims: 45 confirmed, 10 rapes
Location: Liaoning, China
MO: Raped and murdered victims, sometimes post-mortem
Conviction: Executed in 2005
Brief biography:

One of China's most prolific serial killers, Wang Qiang murdered 45 people and committed at least 10 rapes from 1995 to 2003. After years of brutal attacks, some involving post-mortem abuse, he was arrested in 2003. He was sentenced to death and executed in 2005.

Wang Shujin

Aliases: None
DOB: 1967
Nationality: Chinese
Active Years: 1994–1995
Victims: 4 confirmed
Location: Hebei Province, China
MO: Raped and strangled victims
Conviction: Sentenced to death, pending execution
Brief biography:

Wang Shujin committed a string of murders in Hebei, China, raping and strangling four women between 1994 and 1995. He was sentenced to death in 2007. Despite an appeal in 2013, his sentence was upheld, and he remains on death row.

Walker Family Murders

Aliases: None
DOB: -
Nationality: American
Active Years: 1959
Victims: 4
Location: Osprey, Florida, USA
MO: Shooting, sexual assault (Christine Walker)
Conviction: Unsolved; several suspects, no convictions
Brief biography:

On December 20, 1959, the Walker family—Christine, Clifford, and their two children—were found murdered in their Florida home. Christine was sexually assaulted before being shot, and the rest of the family was shot as well. Although there were suspects, no one was ever convicted, and the case remains unsolved.

Wardell Gordon

Aliases: None
DOB: May 8, 1953

Nationality: British
Active Years: 1991–1994
Victims: 3 confirmed
Location: West Midlands, England
MO: Strangulation and staged abduction
Conviction: Life imprisonment for wife's murder
Brief biography:

Gordon Wardell was convicted of the 1994 murder of his wife, Carol, whom he attempted to frame as a victim of a staged abduction. Following a lengthy trial, Wardell was sentenced to life in prison in 1995.

Wardrip Faryion Edward

Aliases: None
DOB: March 6, 1959
Nationality: American
Active Years: 1984–1986
Victims: 5 confirmed
Location: Texas
MO: Rape and stabbing
Conviction: Life sentences plus death sentence
Brief biography:

Faryion Wardrip murdered five women in Texas, primarily targeting young nurses and students, whom he raped and stabbed. DNA evidence in 1999 linked him to these murders, leading to his conviction and subsequent death sentence.

Waters Margaret (The Brixton Baby Farmer)

Aliases: The Brixton Baby Farmer
DOB: 1835
Nationality: British
Active Years: 1860s–1870
Victims: 19+ infants
Location: Brixton, England
MO: Drugging and starving babies
Conviction: Executed by hanging in 1870
Brief biography:

Margaret Waters was a "baby farmer" in 19th-century Britain, responsible for the deaths of at least 19 infants left in her care. Convicted of murdering a baby boy, she was hanged in 1870, leaving behind a notorious legacy.

Watts, Carl Eugene (The Sunday Morning Slasher)

Aliases: The Sunday Morning Slasher
DOB: November 7, 1953
Nationality: American
Active Years: 1974–1982
Victims: Estimated 100+
Location: Michigan, Texas
MO: Stabbing, strangulation, drowning
Conviction: Life imprisonment in 2004
Brief biography:

Carl Eugene Watts, dubbed "The Sunday Morning Slasher," is believed to have killed over 100 women across several states, mainly using stabbing, strangling, and drowning. He was convicted and sentenced to life in prison in Michigan, where he died of cancer in 2007.

Washington D.C. Serial Killer

Active Years: Since November 1996
Victims: 6 known (5 women found dead, 1 missing)
Location: North side neighborhood, Washington D.C.
MO: Unknown

Details: Five women connected to the same neighborhood have been found dead since 1996, with three discovered in gutted buildings. A sixth victim's torso was found in an alley nearby. Darryl Donnell Turner, linked by DNA to two of the murders, was sentenced to life in prison and remains a suspect in the other cases.

Weepy-Voiced Killer (Paul Michael Stephani)

Aliases: The Weepy-Voiced Killer
DOB: September 8, 1944
Nationality: American
Active Years: 1980–1982

Victims: 3 murdered, 2 attempted
Location: Minnesota, Wisconsin
MO: Bludgeoning and stabbing
Conviction: Life imprisonment in 1983
Brief biography:

Paul Michael Stephani, known as the "Weepy-Voiced Killer," would call police in a remorseful voice after his attacks. He was convicted of three murders and two attempted murders, receiving a life sentence in 1983.

West Mesa Murders / Albuquerque Serial Killer

Active Years: 2003-2005
Victims: 18 bodies found, 11 identified
Location: Albuquerque, New Mexico
MO: Kidnapping, murder

Details: A detective aims to identify the victims, referred to as "Somebody's Daughters." Eleven victims have been confirmed, including Monica Candelaria and Syllannia Edwards, most connected to drugs and prostitution. Their remains were discovered buried in a mesa in Albuquerque. The case highlights systemic issues surrounding vulnerable populations.

Weidmann Eugene

Aliases: None
DOB: February 5, 1908
Nationality: German
Active Years: 1935–1937
Victims: 6 confirmed
Location: France
MO: Kidnapping, robbery, shooting
Conviction: Executed by guillotine in 1939
Brief biography:

Eugene Weidmann was a German-born serial killer who operated in France during the 1930s. He lured wealthy tourists, kidnapped them, and killed them for ransom. After confessing to six murders, he was convicted and sentenced to death. His execution by guillotine on June 17, 1939, was the last public execution in France.

Wemmer Pan Killer (Maoupa Cedric Maake)

Aliases: The Wemmer Pan Killer
DOB: 1965
Nationality: South African
Active Years: 1996–1997
Victims: 27 confirmed
Location: Gauteng, South Africa
MO: Shooting, stabbing, bludgeoning
Conviction: Sentenced to 1,159 years in 2000
Brief biography:

Maoupa Cedric Maake, known as the "Wemmer Pan Killer," terrorized Gauteng Province between 1996 and 1997. He targeted victims of any race or gender, using various weapons including guns, knives, and rocks. Maake was convicted of over 100 charges, including 27 murders and 14 rapes, and was sentenced to an astonishing 1,159 years in prison.

Werewolf of Angarsk (Mikhail Viktorovich Popkov)

Aliases: The Werewolf of Angarsk
DOB: March 7, 1964
Nationality: Russian
Active Years: 1992–2010
Victims: 83 confirmed
Location: Angarsk, Irkutsk, Russia
MO: Rape, murder with blunt objects
Conviction: Sentenced to life imprisonment in 2015
Brief biography:

Mikhail Popkov, a former police officer, is among the most prolific serial killers in modern history, known as "The Werewolf of Angarsk." He targeted women he deemed immoral, killing them with weapons like axes and screwdrivers. Initially convicted for 22 murders, his confessions later raised his victim count to 83. He is serving life imprisonment in Russia.

Werewolf Butcher (Jack Owen Spillman III)

Aliases: The Werewolf Butcher
DOB: August 30, 1969
Nationality: American
Active Years: 1994–1995
Victims: 3 confirmed
Location: Washington, USA
MO: Sexual mutilation and murder
Conviction: Life imprisonment in 1996
Brief biography:

Jack Owen Spillman III, known as "The Werewolf Butcher," was convicted of murdering Rita Huffman, her daughter Mandy, and 9-year-old Penny Davis in Washington. He sexually mutilated his victims and posed their bodies provocatively. Spillman was sentenced to life imprisonment without parole in 1996.

Werewolf of Châlons

Aliases: The Werewolf of Châlons
DOB: Unknown
Nationality: French
Active Years: 1590s
Victims: Estimated 10–48
Location: Châlons, France
MO: Cannibalism, murder
Conviction: Burned at the stake in 1598
Brief biography:

The "Werewolf of Châlons," also known as the "Demon Tailor," was a 16th-century French murderer and cannibal who allegedly killed numerous patrons and children. He confessed under torture to between 10 and 48 murders, claiming he dismembered and cannibalized his victims. He was executed by burning in 1598, and his name has since been lost to history.

Werewolf of Dole (Gilles Garnier)

Aliases: The Werewolf of Dole
DOB: c. 1540

Nationality: French
Active Years: 1572
Victims: 4 confirmed
Location: Franche-Comté, France
MO: Strangulation, cannibalism
Conviction: Burned at the stake in 1573
Brief biography:

Gilles Garnier, known as "The Werewolf of Dole," was a French hermit who claimed to transform into a wolf using magic ointment. He confessed to strangling and eating four children. Garnier was convicted of lycanthropy and witchcraft and was burned at the stake in 1573.

Werner Karl Francis

Aliases: None
DOB: 1950
Nationality: American
Active Years: 1969–1971
Victims: 3 confirmed
Location: Santa Clara County, USA
MO: Stabbing
Conviction: Sentenced to life imprisonment in 1971
Brief biography:

Karl Francis Werner was convicted of murdering three teenage girls in California between 1969 and 1971. His victims were brutally stabbed multiple times. Although initially a suspect in the Zodiac killings, it was proven he had no connection to those crimes. He was sentenced to life imprisonment for the murders.

Wayne Adam Ford

Aliases: Wayward Wayne
DOB: c. 1948
Nationality: Canadian
Active Years: 1969–1971
Victims: 4
Location: Montreal, Quebec & Calgary, Alberta

MO: Rape, strangulation, biting victims' breasts
Conviction: Life imprisonment, died of skin cancer in 2006
Brief biography:

Wayne Adam Ford, also known as "Wayward Wayne," is a serial killer who confessed to murdering four women between 1997 and 1998. He would strangle his victims, dismember their bodies, and dump the remains in remote locations. Ford turned himself in to police with a severed breast in his pocket, leading to his arrest and life sentence.

Wayne Clifford Boden

Aliases: The Vampire Rapist
DOB: c. 1948
Nationality: Canadian
Active Years: 1969–1971
Victims: 4
Location: Montreal, Quebec & Calgary, Alberta
MO: Rape, strangulation, biting victims' breasts
Conviction: Life imprisonment, died of skin cancer in 2006
Brief biography:

Wayne Clifford Boden, the "Vampire Rapist," was a Canadian serial killer who raped and murdered four women from 1969 to 1971. He was notorious for biting his victims' breasts, leaving bite-mark evidence that led to his conviction. Boden was sentenced to life imprisonment and died of cancer in 2006, becoming the first person convicted in North America using bite-mark evidence.

Wayne Nathan Nance

Aliases: None
DOB: 1955
Nationality: American
Active Years: 1974–1986
Victims: 6
Location: Montana, USA
MO: Bludgeoning, stabbing, shooting
Conviction: Killed during a home invasion
Brief biography:

Wayne Nance, also known as the Missoula Mauler, was an American serial killer suspected of murdering six people in Montana between 1974 and 1986. He was killed in 1986 during a home invasion when one of his intended victims managed to overpower him and shoot him in self-defense.

William Dale Archerd

Aliases: None
DOB: 1912
Nationality: American
Active Years: 1950s-1960s
Victims: 3
Location: California, USA
MO: Poisoning with insulin
Conviction: Sentenced to death, commuted to life
Brief biography:

William Dale Archerd, a former pharmacist, was convicted of murdering three family members by injecting them with insulin, leading to hypoglycemic comas and eventual death. His victims included his wife and two relatives, all killed to collect life insurance money. Archerd was sentenced to death in 1967, but his sentence was later commuted to life imprisonment. His cold, calculated method of killing using a medical substance made him one of California's most infamous murderers of the time.

William Devin Howell

Aliases: N/A
DOB: February 11, 1970
Nationality: American
Active Years: 2003
Victims: 7
Location: New Britain, Connecticut
MO: Rape and murder; bodies buried in a wooded area
Conviction: Convicted of 6 counts of murder; life sentence
Brief biography:

William Devin Howell is Connecticut's most prolific serial killer. In 2003, he killed seven people, including six women and one man, hiding the bodies behind a shopping center in New Britain. While he claimed that rape was his primary motivation, he killed his victims to prevent them from reporting him to the police. Howell's chilling nonchalance during interviews demonstrated his complete lack of remorse. He was convicted of six murders and sentenced to life in prison.

Weepy-Voiced Killer (Paul Michael Stephani)

Aliases: The Weepy-Voiced Killer
DOB: September 8, 1944
Nationality: American
Active Years: 1980–1982
Victims: 3 confirmed, 2 attempted
Location: Minnesota, USA
MO: Stabbing, bludgeoning
Conviction: Sentenced to 40 years in 1983
Brief biography:

Paul Michael Stephani, known as the "Weepy-Voiced Killer," gained notoriety for calling the police after his attacks, weeping and expressing remorse. His crime spree included the murders of three women and the attempted murder of two others in Minnesota between 1980 and 1982. Stephani was apprehended after a surviving victim identified him. He was sentenced to 40 years in prison and died of cancer in 1998.

Weidenbroeker Helmut

Aliases: None
DOB: 1965
Nationality: German
Active Years: 1982–1986
Victims: 5 confirmed
Location: Aachen, Germany
MO: Strangulation
Conviction: Sentenced to life imprisonment in 1987
Brief biography:

Helmut Weidenbroeker was a German chemist who murdered five women in Aachen between 1982 and 1986. His victims were young women, most of whom he strangled. Although suspected in several other killings, Weidenbroeker was only convicted of one murder and sentenced to life imprisonment in 1987.

Wenzinger Gerd

Aliases: The Havel Ripper
DOB: 1943
Nationality: German
Active Years: 1990s
Victims: 17 confirmed
Location: Germany, Brazil
MO: Torture, mutilation, dissection
Conviction: Committed suicide in 1997
Brief biography:

Gerd Wenzinger, known as "The Havel Ripper," was a notorious German serial killer and torturer who murdered at least 17 women during the 1990s. Wenzinger filmed some of his gruesome acts of torture and mutilation. He was arrested in Brazil and later hanged himself in his prison cell in 1997 before facing trial.

Webb Dennis Duane

Aliases: None
DOB: 1952
Nationality: American
Active Years: 1973–1987
Victims: 8 confirmed
Location: Texas, California, USA
MO: Burglary, rape, murder
Conviction: Sentenced to death in 1988
Brief biography:

Dennis Duane Webb was a notorious American serial killer and outlaw biker who confessed to eight murders between 1973 and 1987. He also raped both male and female victims. Webb was convicted of the 1987 murders of Lori and John Rainwater in California and was sentenced to death in 1988. He died of undisclosed causes in 2016 while on death row.

Webb Emanuel Lovell

Aliases: None
DOB: 1966
Nationality: American
Active Years: 1990–1994
Victims: 4 confirmed
Location: Bridgeport, Connecticut, USA
MO: Rape, strangulation
Conviction: Sentenced to 60 years in 1996
Brief biography:

Emanuel Lovell Webb was convicted of raping and murdering four women in Bridgeport, Connecticut, between 1990 and 1994. His victims were found mutilated or disfigured, and he was eventually tied to the crimes through DNA evidence. Webb was sentenced to 60 years in prison in 1996 and is currently serving his sentence at MacDougall-Walker Correctional Institution.

Weber Jeanne

Aliases: None
DOB: October 7, 1874
Nationality: French
Active Years: 1905–1908
Victims: 10 confirmed
Location: Paris, France
MO: Strangulation of children
Conviction: Committed suicide in 1918
Brief biography:

Jeanne Weber, a French serial killer, strangled at least 10 children, including her own, between 1905 and 1908. Despite being acquitted in her initial trials due to lack of evidence, she continued to murder. Weber was eventually arrested and sent to a mental institution, where she hanged herself in 1918.

Weidmann Eugene

Aliases: None
DOB: February 5, 1908

Nationality: German
Active Years: 1935–1937
Victims: 6 confirmed
Location: France
MO: Kidnapping, robbery, murder
Conviction: Guillotined in 1939
Brief biography:

Eugene Weidmann was a German criminal who committed a series of murders during robberies and ransom kidnappings in France between 1935 and 1937. He was arrested, found guilty, and sentenced to death. Weidmann was guillotined outside the Prison Saint-Pierre in Versailles on June 17, 1939. He was the last person to be publicly executed in France.

Wemmer Pan Killer (Maoupa Cedric Maake)

Aliases: Wemmer Pan Killer
DOB: 1965
Nationality: South African
Active Years: 1996–1997
Victims: 27 confirmed
Location: Gauteng Province, South Africa
MO: Shooting, stabbing, bludgeoning
Conviction: Sentenced to 1,159 years in 2000
Brief biography:

Maoupa Cedric Maake, known as the Wemmer Pan Killer, terrorized South Africa's Gauteng Province between 1996 and 1997, killing 27 people. His victims ranged from shopkeepers and taxi drivers to couples and women. Maake used guns, knives, and blunt objects to carry out his murders. In 2000, he was convicted of 27 murders, along with numerous other charges, and sentenced to over 1,000 years in prison.

William Burke & William Hare

Aliases: Burke & Hare
DOB: Burke: c. 1792
Nationality: Scottish-Irish
Active Years: 1827–1828
Victims: 17 known victims
Location: Edinburgh, Scotland
MO: Suffocation; sold bodies for dissection
Conviction: Burke: Executed; Hare: Immunity for confession
Brief biography:

Burke and Hare were notorious serial killers who sold the bodies of their victims to medical schools for dissection in the 1820s. Operating in Edinburgh, they lured mostly vulnerable individuals to their lodging house, got them intoxicated, and then suffocated them. The bodies were sold to Dr. Robert Knox, an anatomist. Burke was eventually arrested and executed, while Hare was granted immunity in exchange for testifying against his partner. This case led to significant changes in the laws surrounding the procurement of cadavers for medical research.

William Palmer

Aliases: The Rugeley Poisoner
DOB: August 6, 1824
Nationality: British
Active Years: 1840s–1855
Victims: 1 confirmed, suspected 14+
Location: England (Staffordshire)
MO: Poisoning with strychnine
Conviction: Executed by hanging, 1856
Brief biography:

William Palmer, known as "The Rugeley Poisoner," was a British doctor and serial killer who poisoned his victims for financial gain. Palmer was responsible for a series of suspicious deaths, including that of John Parsons Cook, his wife, and several family members. His weapon of choice was strychnine, a deadly poison. Palmer was convicted of murder in 1856 and executed by hanging. His case is one of the most infamous in British legal history.

William Paul Thompson

Aliases: N/A
DOB: 1937
Nationality: American
Active Years: 1983–1984
Victims: 6 confirmed
Location: New York, Kansas, California, Nevada
MO: Contract killings and personal conflicts
Conviction: Executed by lethal injection, 1989
Brief biography:

William Paul Thompson was a contract killer and murderer who killed six men in 1983–1984. He was convicted of two murders in California and sentenced to death in Nevada. His crimes included personal conflicts and murders for hire. Thompson was executed by lethal injection at Nevada State Prison on June 19, 1989.

Willie Kimmritz

Aliases: Terror of Brandenburg Forest
DOB: June 26, 1912
Nationality: German
Active Years: 1948
Victims: 4 confirmed, 23 rapes
Location: Brandenburg Forest, Germany
MO: Rape and murder of women, robbery
Conviction: Executed by guillotine in 1950
Brief biography:

Willie Kimmritz, known as the "Terror of Brandenburg Forest," was a German serial killer, rapist, and burglar who preyed on women in the post-World War II years. Arrested in 1948, Kimmritz confessed to numerous rapes and murders in the Brandenburg area. He was sentenced to death and executed by guillotine in 1950. His crimes left a chilling legacy in postwar Germany.

Wolfgang Abel and Marco Furlan

Aliases: Nazis
DOB: Abel: March 25, 1959; Furlan: January 16, 1959

Nationality: Italian
Active Years: 1977–1984
Victims: Estimated 28
Location: Italy
MO: Murder of "sinners" via various methods
Conviction: Both: 27 years imprisonment
Brief biography:

Wolfgang Abel and Marco Furlan were Nazi sympathizers who embarked on a killing spree across Italy from 1977 to 1984. They claimed to be purging society of "sinners" and killed drug addicts, prostitutes, and homeless people using methods like arson and lethal injection. They were captured and sentenced to 27 years in prison each.

Chapter Twenty-Two: Y-List

Yakima Reservation Unsolved Murders

Active Years: 1982-1992
Victims: 32 unsolved murders, 13 outlined
Location: Yakima Reservation, Washington
MO: Various methods including strangulation and blunt force

Details: A Native American woman was found murdered in December 1992, marking the 13th victim in a decade of killings on the Yakima Reservation. Notable cases include Sheila Pearl Lewis, who died of internal injuries, and several others with causes ranging from drowning to homicide. Many of the cases remain open and unsolved, highlighting ongoing concerns about violence against women in marginalized communities.

Yahweh Ben Yahweh

Aliases: Mitchell Hulon Jr.
DOB: October 27, 1935
Nationality: American
Active Years: 1980s
Victims: 25+ victims, including defectors
Location: Liberty City, Florida
MO: Murder of "white devils," decapitation
Conviction: Convicted of conspiracy, released in 2001

Brief biography:

Yahweh Ben Yahweh, born Mitchell Hulon Jr., was the leader of the Nation of Yahweh, a racist cult responsible for the murders of at least 25 individuals, including cult defectors and perceived enemies. His cult targeted "white devils" and committed various brutal murders. Yahweh and six others were convicted on federal conspiracy charges in 1992. He was released from prison in 2001 and died of prostate cancer in 2007.

Yang Shuming

Aliases: N/A
DOB: Unknown
Nationality: Chinese
Active Years: 1993-2004
Victims: 9 murdered, 3 assaulted
Location: Yangquan, Shanxi Province, China
MO: Murders and assaults during night and bad weather
Conviction: Arrested August 3, 2006
Brief biography:

Yang Shuming was a serial killer in Yangquan, China, responsible for the murder of nine women and the assault of three others between 1993 and 2004. His attacks took place at night or during bad weather, in the area around the Majiaping mine. Yang was finally arrested on August 3, 2006, and charged with the murders.

Yang Xinhai

Aliases: Monster Killer
DOB: July 29, 1968
Nationality: Chinese
Active Years: 2000-2003
Victims: 67 murdered, 23 raped
Location: Multiple provinces, China
MO: Breaking into homes, killing with axes, hammers, shovels
Conviction: Executed by firing squad on February 14, 2004
Brief biography:

Yang Xinhai, known as the "Monster Killer," terrorized several provinces in China between 2000 and 2003. He broke into homes at night, killing entire families with axes, hammers, and shovels, and raped many of his victims. Yang was arrested in 2003 and confessed to 65 murders and 23 rapes. He was sentenced to death and executed in February 2004.

Yavuz Yapicioglu

Aliases: N/A
DOB: 1967
Nationality: Turkish
Active Years: 1994-2002
Victims: 18 confirmed, possibly 40
Location: Turkey
MO: Multiple murders, arson, assault
Conviction: Sentenced to life imprisonment in 2003
Brief biography:

Yavuz Yapicioglu is a Turkish serial killer and arsonist who murdered at least 18 people, possibly as many as 40, between 1994 and 2002. He committed his first murders in 1994 and continued to kill, assault, and set fires over the years. Yapicioglu was arrested in 2002, declared criminally liable for his crimes, and sentenced to life imprisonment in 2003.

Yaghoub Ali Mirshekari

Aliases: Yellow Scorpion
DOB: 1957
Nationality: Iranian
Active Years: 2004
Victims: 10 truck drivers
Location: Zahedan, Iran
MO: Murdered truck drivers, stole their vehicles
Conviction: Hanged publicly in Zahedan on June 12, 2005
Brief biography:

Yaghoub Ali Mirshekari, known as the "Yellow Scorpion," was the leader of a group that murdered 10 truck drivers in Zahedan, Iran, in 2004. He, along with family members, killed drivers to steal their trucks, which they then sold in Pakistan. Mirshekari was convicted and publicly hanged in 2005.

Yoo Young-Chul

Aliases: N/A
DOB: April 18, 1970
Nationality: South Korean
Active Years: 2003-2004

Victims: 20 confirmed, possibly 26
Location: Seoul, South Korea
MO: Hammer murders, dismemberment, cannibalism
Conviction: Sentenced to death in December 2004
Brief biography:

Yoo Young-Chul was a South Korean serial killer responsible for the murders of at least 20 people between 2003 and 2004, including wealthy elderly people and female prostitutes. He beat his victims with a hammer, mutilated and dismembered some, and even cannibalized parts of their bodies. Yoo was sentenced to death in December 2004.

Yuri Anufrievich Ivanov

Aliases: Ust-Kamenogorsk Maniac
DOB: 1956
Nationality: Kazakh
Active Years: 1986–1987
Victims: 16 confirmed
Location: Kazakhstan
MO: Raped and strangled women
Conviction: Executed by firing squad, 1989
Brief biography:

Yuri Ivanov, known as the Ust-Kamenogorsk Maniac, was a Kazakh serial killer who targeted women in Kazakhstan in 1986–1987. He killed women who spoke ill of men or their husbands, raping and strangling them. Ivanov was arrested after a 16-year-old victim's body was found, and forensic evidence tied him to multiple murders. He was sentenced to death and executed by firing squad in 1989.

Yves "Apache" Trudeau

Aliases: Apache
DOB: February 4, 1946
Nationality: Canadian
Active Years: 1973–1985
Victims: 43 confirmed
Location: Quebec, Canada
MO: Shooting, bombings, strangulation

Conviction: Life imprisonment (paroled in 1994)
Brief biography:

Yves "Apache" Trudeau was a notorious hitman for the Hells Angels motorcycle gang in Quebec, Canada. Between 1973 and 1985, Trudeau murdered 43 people, many of whom were rivals of the gang or those who crossed the gang in the drug trade. His methods included shootings and bombings. In 1985, fearing for his life, Trudeau became a government witness and provided key testimony that led to the conviction of several Hells Angels members. In exchange, he received a life sentence with the possibility of parole, and was released in 1994 under a new identity. He died of cancer in 2008.

Chapter Twenty-Three: Z-List

Zaven Sarkisovich Almazyan

Aliases: None
DOB: 1930
Nationality: Russian
Active Years: 1980s
Victims: 5 confirmed
Location: Soviet Union
MO: Strangulation
Conviction: Sentenced to death

Brief biography:

Zaven Sarkisovich Almazyan was a Russian serial killer who terrorized parts of the Soviet Union in the 1980s. He was convicted of strangling five women, whom he often targeted in isolated areas. Almazyan was sentenced to death in 1987 after a trial that captured widespread media attention due to the brutality of his crimes. He was executed by firing squad shortly after his conviction.

Zebra Killers

Aliases: Death Angels (Group)
DOB: N/A
Nationality: American
Active Years: 1973-1974
Victims: 15 murdered, 8 injured/raped
Location: San Francisco, California
MO: Random racially motivated killings, torture, shootings
Conviction: Four members sentenced to life in prison
Brief biography:

The "Zebra Killers" or "Death Angels" were a splinter group of Black Muslims responsible for racially motivated murders in San Francisco between 1973 and 1974. They killed 15 white people and injured several others in random attacks.

One of the gunmen, Anthony Harris, turned informant, leading to the arrest and conviction of four members. They were sentenced to life imprisonment, and the case heightened racial tensions in the area.

Zhou Wen

Aliases: Taxi Demon
DOB: 1965
Nationality: Chinese
Active Years: 2001–2003
Victims: 6
Location: Anshan, Liaoning Province, China
MO: Strangled female passengers and disposed of bodies
Conviction: Arrested in 2003, no trial information available
Brief biography:

Zhou Wen, also known as the Taxi Demon, was a Chinese serial killer active in Anshan, Liaoning Province, China. He murdered at least six women between 2001 and 2003, strangling them in his taxi before dumping their bodies in the wastelands surrounding the city. Wen harbored a deep hatred for women after his wife had an abortion without his consent. After his arrest in 2003, he handed over a diary detailing his crimes, aiding police in locating the bodies of his victims. There is no clear information about his trial or sentence.

Zhang Jun

Aliases: N/A
DOB: August 5, 1966
Nationality: Chinese
Active Years: 1993-2000
Victims: 28 murders
Location: Multiple locations, China
MO: Robbery, multiple homicides
Conviction: Executed on May 20, 2001
Brief biography:

Zhang Jun was a notorious Chinese serial killer and robber who committed multiple murders during his robbery spree between 1993 and 2000. He was involved in numerous violent crimes and killed several people during his heists. Zhang was arrested in 2000, convicted, and executed on May 20, 2001.

Zhang Xianguang

Aliases: N/A
DOB: 1965
Nationality: Chinese
Active Years: 1993-2006
Victims: 10 murdered
Location: Heilongjiang, China
MO: Robbery and murder
Conviction: Executed in 2006
Brief biography:

Zhang Xianguang was a Chinese serial killer who murdered at least 10 people over a span of 3.5 years. He was involved in several high-value robberies totaling millions of yuan. He was arrested in 2006 and executed for his crimes that same year.

Zhao Zhihong

Aliases: N/A
DOB: September 5, 1972
Nationality: Chinese
Active Years: 1996-2005
Victims: 11 murdered, 23 rapes
Location: Inner Mongolia, China
MO: Sexual assault, robbery, murder
Conviction: Executed on July 30, 2019
Brief biography:

Zhao Zhihong, a farmer from Inner Mongolia, raped and murdered 11 women between 1996 and 2005. He was arrested in 2005 and confessed to his crimes. Notably, another man was wrongfully executed for some of Zhao's murders in 1996. Zhao was executed on July 30, 2019.

Zhou Kehua

Aliases: N/A
DOB: February 6, 1970
Nationality: Chinese
Active Years: 2005-2012
Victims: 10 murdered
Location: Chongqing, China
MO: Armed robbery, shooting
Conviction: Killed by police on August 14, 2012
Brief biography:

Zhou Kehua was a notorious Chinese serial killer and armed robber who murdered at least 10 people during his criminal spree from 2005 to 2012. He was a former mercenary soldier in Burma. Zhou was shot and killed by police in Chongqing after a massive manhunt on August 14, 2012.

Conclusion

Whoa. Hold on a second. Take a deep breath. We've just emerged from a deep, dark rabbit hole, my friend. And let's be real, we might need a shower and a stiff drink (or maybe something a little stronger) to wash away the grime of the stories we've just uncovered.

Did you ever think we'd be discussing cannibal lampshades, kimchi-scented body parts, or a killer who chilled with his victims' corpses like it was just another Netflix marathon? I mean, come on! The human race is capable of some seriously messed-up stuff.

But here's the thing that's even more mind-blowing than the depravity itself: these aren't just campfire tales or horror movies. These are real people, real victims, real families shattered by unimaginable acts. It's enough to make you want to lock your doors forever and never trust a soul again.

But before you spiral into a pit of existential dread, remember this: we also encountered incredible strength and resilience. We learned about survivors who outsmarted their attackers, investigators who cracked codes and chased shadows, and families who never gave up on the search for truth.

And guess what? We're part of that community now. We're the ones who refuse to turn away from the darkness, who seek to understand the monsters among us, not just to satisfy a morbid curiosity, but to arm ourselves with knowledge. Knowledge is power, right? And maybe, just maybe, by shining a light on these twisted tales, we can prevent future tragedies.

So, yeah, the world can be a scary place. But it's also a world filled with brave souls fighting for justice, for truth, for a little bit of light in the face of unimaginable darkness.

As you close this book, remember the victims, honor their memories, and never stop questioning the shadows. The world of true crime is a twisted, terrifying, and utterly unforgettable journey. And we've just scratched the surface.

The End...for now. (But let's be real, the nightmares are just beginning.)

Other Books in The Series

The Ultimate True Crime Trivia: 330 Intriguing Questions and Answers

By K. Murdle.

Original Serial Killer & True Crime Trivia Book.

By K. Murdle.

The Ultimate True Crime Activity Book: 100 puzzles. Serial Killers Coloring Pages, Word Search, Crosswords, Trivia, Mazes, Word Scramble and much more!

By K. Murdle.

All Books are on Amazon.

Thanks

Made in the USA
Las Vegas, NV
13 December 2025

36351408R00109